EXPO

trade fair stand design

RotoVision

EXPO

trade fair stand design

Conway Lloyd Morgan

PRO *Graphics*

A RotoVision Book
Published and distributed by RotoVision SA
Rue du Bugnon 7
CH-1299 Crans-Près-Céligny
Switzerland

RotoVision SA, Sales & Production Office
Sheridan House, 112/116A Western Road
Hove, East Sussex BN3 1DD, UK

Tel: +44 (0) 1273 72 72 68
Fax: +44 (0) 1273 72 72 69

Distributed to the trade in the United States by:
Watson-Guptill Publications
1515 Broadway
New York, NY 10036

Copyright © RotoVision SA 1997

All rights reserved. No part of this publication may be reproduced, stored in a retrieval system or transmitted in any form or by any means, electronic, mechanical, photocopying, recording or otherwise, without permission of the copyright holder.

The products, trademarks, logos and proprietary shapes used in this book are copyrighted or otherwise protected by legislation and cannot be reproduced without the permission of the holder of the rights.

ISBN 2-88046-263-0

Book design by Lindsey Johns at The Design Revolution

Production and separations by ProVision Pte. Ltd. in Singapore

Tel: +65 334 7720
Fax: +65 334 7721

CONTENTS

Introduction — 6–9

Planning an expo installation — 10–11

Ford – The overall Euro view — 12–21

SECTION 1: Starting out — 22

Vero & Didou – Staging the shell — 23–26

Azur Environmental – Celebrating the island — 27–30

Emašport – Pairing the clients — 31–34

Hoxan – Bridging the gap — 35–41

SECTION 2: Designing into Space — 42

Olivetti – Launching David against Goliath — 43–46

Philips – Pixelating the logo — 47–54

Mizuno – Olympic powerhouse — 55–58

Trinova Vickers – Toys for big boys — 59–62

America Online – Selling the invisible — 63–66

Reggiani – Light, shade and space — 67–70

Golden Books – Reaffirming reading — 71–74

GT Interactive – The heavenly product — 75–79

SECTION 3: Presenting the Client — 80

Kartell – Going with the flow — 81–86

Microsoft – Multiple presentations, multiple markets — 87–92

Mercedes-Benz – Éppur' si muove — 93–98

Intel – Marking the sponsor's space — 99–106

Ericsson – Outreach and acrobatics — 107–114

Virgin Interactive – Marketing the medieval — 115–123

SECTION 4: Beyond the Stand — 124

Pilkington – Through the glass clearly — 125–130

Fox Video – Taking the show on the road — 131–136

Gardner Merchant – The permanent food event — 137–142

Conclusion — 143–144

Tango – Person to person with style — 145–154

Acknowledgments — 155

List of designers — 156–157

Index — 158–159

INTRODUCTION

Traditional market stalls offer variety and liveliness

Think of a street market: lots of people moving from stall to stall, some with a specific shopping list in hand, some avid for bargains, some just curious to see what is new and different. Some sellers shout their wares, some rely on the repartee between salesman and customer, some expect the discerning buyer to look at prices and then choose. Among the pleasures of shopping in a market are the variety of goods on offer, the differences in presentation, the sense that all the other people here are enjoying it too. A trade fair is, in many ways, like a market. It may be indoors, in a grand hotel or a specially designed conference center, and it may be open to the public or just to professionals. The stands may be simple or sophisticated, run up from whatever was to hand at the last minute or planned months in advance. But the human atmosphere of a trade fair is, like a market, a mixture of the determined, the curious and the committed.

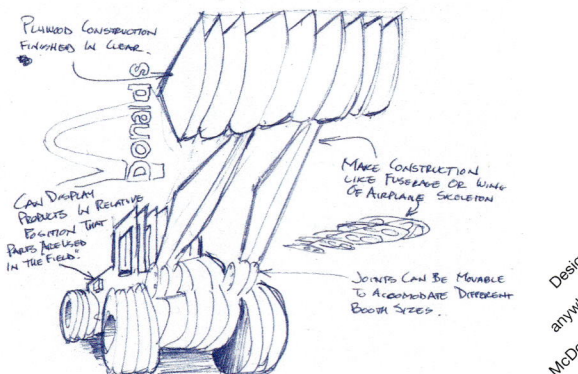

Designing can start anywhere, even on a McDonald's napkin

Trade fair shows are today an integral part of any company's marketing strategy. They provide opportunities for showing new products, for greeting and meeting potential customers, and for talking to established contacts. A fair is also an opportunity to see and sense what competitors are doing, and how they are doing it. For all these reasons, making a positive appearance at a trade fair, whether for the general public or an invited professional audience, is now established as a key and necessary way of doing business.

3-D computer modeling can be used to present the design to the client

The trade fair is thus a forum for quality time between the firm and its market. This means that whatever the size of the stand or the nature of the event, the final design has to be immediately responsive. This places a large number of demands on the designer of trade fair stands – examining how those demands have been met is the main aim of this book. But first some general principles.

Trade fair design is highly costly to the client. Taking marketeers and sales personnel from behind their desks to man a stand costs the client money and time, over and above the actual cost of the stand itself.

Trade fair design is design against time. Not only is there normally only a short space of time to build a stand, the attention span of most visitors is short. So the designer needs to plan and organize the design not only for rapid erection and construction, but also to extend a rapid and clear invitation to the visitor to step aboard the stand.

Expo design centers on the visitor experience at the stand itself.

Trade fair design is both open and closed: within the fair as a whole the stand needs to be visible, literally remarkable, and once inside the stand the visitor must come away with a clear experience of the visit.

Trade fair design is both temporary and permanent: the stand is up for a few days, but the memory of it stays in the customer's mind much longer.

Trade fair design is continuous, not unique: the statements made by a stand need to be reinforced by the rest of the client company's behavior, and so linked to other graphic promotions and advertising.

The design process needs stages of visualization to determine the best solution.

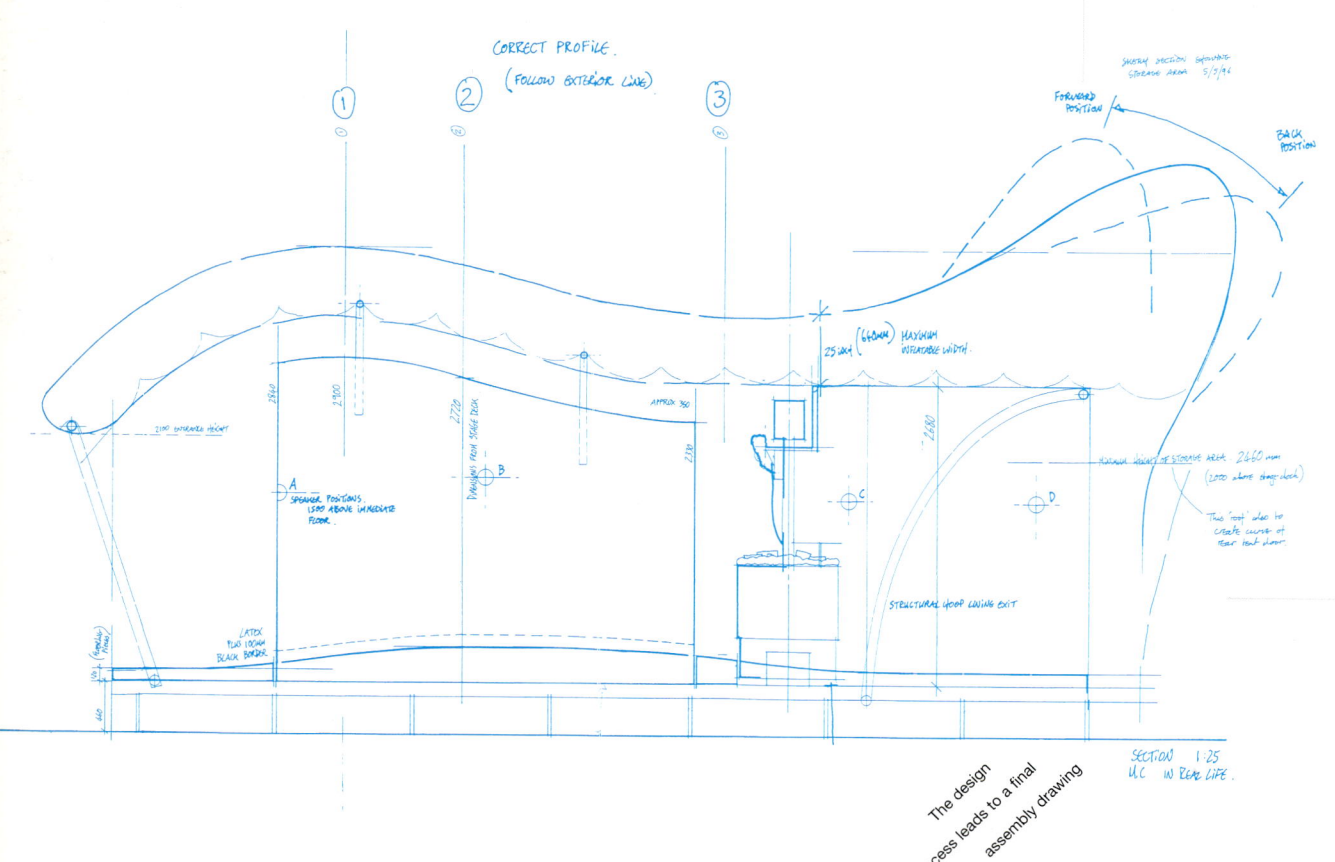

The design process leads to a final assembly drawing

Taking the trade fair to the street in the form of a carnival display

Trade fair design demands organizational skills: not just in executing the stand design in final, physical form, but in supplying support, whether through printed or video materials for presentations, communication and computer facilities, hospitality areas, stand staff preparation, press packs and promotional literature and gifts. The designer needs to play a coordinating role in all these areas.

Trade fair design is part of marketing: so the better the designer understands the marketing strategy of the company, the better the stand design will serve those needs. One of his friends described the legendary American pilot Chuck Yeager (the first man to fly at supersonic speed) as 'the only guy I met who ever really fitted inside an aircraft'. By this he meant that Yeager flew at one with his plane, responding totally to it as if part of the machine. A good designer needs to have the same relationship with the client, to be able to see the world through the client's eyes, as well as bringing specialist skills to bear in solving the client's brief. The designer has wider responsibilities as well, especially to be socially aware, to be just in the choice of materials and form, which are equally important. And in the heady and expensive context of trade fair design, where the client is face to face with the public, using these abilities well becomes an exciting and fascinating challenge.

Attention to detail (here at the Ericsson stand at CeBIT) can make or mar the impression created by the stand

Planning an expo installation

CLIENT

Client

Contact name

Name of fair

| **Type of fair** | Professional | Semi-professional | Public | Attendance |
| **Dates** | Set-up period | Duration | Strike-down | Stand storage after fair |

TECHNICAL

| **Stand size and type** | Presentation areas | Meeting areas | Hospitality areas | |

Existing materials/stand

Furniture/fittings

| **Technical support** | Video | Audio | Computers | IT links |

PRODUCT

Products to be presented

Stand personnel

| **Stand facilities** | Communications | Lighting | Control systems | Storage areas |
| | Maintenance and cleaning | | | |

CORPORATE

Corporate logo

Corporate colors

MARKETING

Marketing strapline for fair

Marketing strapline for products

Theme for stand

SUPPORT

| **Supporting material** | Video | Film | Audio | Printed matter |
| | Press pack | | | |

Promotional gifts

Staff uniforms/badges

Other

The check-list shows some of the main considerations to bear in mind when planning the design of a trade fair event. In the following sections you will see how designers have tackled some of the questions raised here. This list shows the main subjects that need to be covered in a briefing meeting with a client. Each subject will itself need further notes, drawings, designs and discussions. See this as a framework for planning, not a complete solution.

Client
This section gives you the baseline information about the event you are designing for, the time-scale for the job, and the number of visitors and type of visitors you need to provide for.

Technical
The stand size and type will help you define how different areas on the stand are allocated, for display (presentation areas), for greeting and discussion (meeting areas), or for entertaining (hospitality areas). You also need to decide how the stand is to be furnished, and whether support systems such as video displays, sound effects or computers – either for visitors or for stand personnel to use – need to be included in the final design. Today many companies are also using IT links to off-site locations.

Product
The stand product is both the objects or services being offered by the client, and in another sense, the personnel and facilities which support this presentation. Ensuring the managed organization of the stand is as much part of the designer's overall brief as getting the 'look' of the stand right.

Corporate
It is important for the designer to be aware of the client's corporate policy regarding the use and placement of logos – whether corporate or for product ranges or services – and whether there are associated corporate colors that need to be incorporated into the final design proposal. This aspect links directly into the marketing message for the stand.

Marketing
It is the designer's duty to support and enhance the central marketing concept for the product or services presented on the stand, and to link this with a wider commitment to the corporate marketing operation of the client. In most cases, these requirements will play a defining factor in creating the theme for the stand, and even in cases where the designer has a wholly free hand it is best to respect the overall marketing approach of the client.

Support
Since a proper design concept for an expo event should not be limited to the physical appearance of the stand, it is always worth knowing what supporting material the client may need – a video or film to present a new product, new publicity leaflets or catalogs, and a press pack for visiting journalists, for example. Ideally, the same team should have design responsibility for all these elements so as to ensure that the message they put across individually is cohesive with the whole. The same applies to promotional gifts, give-aways, staff uniforms and badges.

client: Ford of Europe, Brentwood, Essex, UK

designer: Imagination, London, UK

product/service: Automobiles

fair: European Motor Shows (Birmingham, Geneva, Frankfurt, Paris)

date: 1996–1997

The major international motor shows around the world are widely regarded as being the most important events on the fair calendar, partly in terms of the number of visitors, but also in terms of the industry itself. They provide an opportunity not only for showcasing new products, but also for presenting, often through special 'show vehicles', a future vision of the company concerned. Motor shows also attract all levels of attention: the professional customers – dealers, agents, fleet managers and exporters – in particular, but also the press – a key element in the marketing of cars, vans and trucks – and the general public, from private individuals passionate about cars, to those who just want an entertaining day out. And for motor industry executives the shows are an important international contact point. Just as the first night of a new play or musical can settle its future fate, so a successful motor show presentation can spell success or disaster for a new vehicle launch.

client: **Ford of Europe**

fair: **European Motor Shows**

stand size: **Two-level island stand, sizes from 1,500 square meters (approx. 5000 square feet)**

total production time: **Continuously evolving project**

FORD OF EUROPE

Over the last 15 years, the London-based group *Imagination* has evolved a consistently successful approach to design and communications, mainly by seeing the two disciplines as completely interrelated, and in turn linked to the wider aims of its clients rather than a specific brief. Ford UK and Ford of Europe have both been major clients for all sorts of events and presentations, as well as motor shows, for much of that time. The challenge facing *Imagination* for the 1996–1997 European motor show season was not only to create a successful environment for presenting new vehicles – notably the Ford Ka, Puma and Mondeo – but also to create a design metaphor and system that could be applied to all Ford's major European show presentations.

General view of the stand at Birmingham

Launching the Ka

Access to the upper area

client: **Ford of Europe**

fair: **European Motor Shows**

The decision to implement a Ford of Europe Motor Show Program was not at all just a matter of economics of scale. True, by using a similar module for all the major European shows, planning and presentation could be streamlined. But more important was the notion that Ford should present itself with a **consistent brand image** across Europe, while still recognizing local market or regional differences. This was the task presented to *Imagination*, who accepted it in full – booking the sites, the complete stand design and implementation, incorporating films, graphics, technical exhibits, promotional items and print, right down to the menus for the in-stand restaurant. The final version of the project is thus the fruit of nearly a year's research and development, alongside the existing program of fairs and events created for Ford by *Imagination*.

The Ka Café at Birmingham

The creation of a project of this scale requires three main stages. First is the conception of the structure. This is partly based on the practical requirements of the stand, partly on the designer's understanding of the client's wishes and the brief, and partly on the designer's imagination and skill. It leads to sketches to visualize particular features, functional diagrams to analyze usage requirements, and ideas documents to develop with the client. These initial ideas are evolved through discussion with the client either directly or with the agent's dedicated client-handling account team working alongside the designers, through more detailed models, both in physical form and on the computer, and by formal analysis. This **continuous redefinition** of the brief towards a final form demands communication skills and clear understanding from the designers – establishing an open and aware dialog with the client is the key to success. The final phase, with the design parameters well established, is the detailed costing, planning and commissioning of the event. The cost and logistical aspects of earlier designs will have been considered during those stages, mainly by the account team, but they now have to be brought to a final design. This in turn demands organizational and planning skills from the whole team.

Projects of this scale require organizational and planning skills, as well as design imagination.

client: **Ford of Europe**

fair: **European Motor Shows**

Technical presentation for the Mondeo

The basic requirements of the client brief were to present the current range of cars, both visually and technically, in a static display. They also had to create a presentation theater for any new models, and provide facilities for hospitality and for individual and group meetings. The design that evolved was for a stand with a core section on two levels, with the VIP lounge, offices and meeting rooms on the upper level. The static displays are set around the edge of the stand or on the front 'apron', with the presentation theater area, seating up to 200, usually ranged against the back wall of the stand.

'Edge architecture.'

'Edge architecture' at work

client: **Ford of Europe**

fair: **European Motor Shows**

Formula 1 racing car on display

Historic cars on display at Birmingham

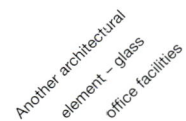

Another architectural element – glass office facilities

Derived from the new design styling of Ford's cars, *Imagination* conceived the concept of 'edge architecture' as the design model for the new stands. This makes the stand a **primary corporate statement**, using large wall blocks in a vibrant blue color to mark out areas on the stand. This approach makes the stand both identifiable at a distance, and invites the visitor to explore the stand, as the ramps on which cars are displayed are behind the walls. Other architectural elements are large glass display blocks containing, for example, a Formula 1 racing car, or a video wall. Placing the presentation area against the back wall, among cafés and refreshment booths, also draws the visitor in, glimpsing the various elements across the gaps in the blue walls.

client: **Ford of Europe**

fair: **European Motor Shows**

The design ethos behind the new approach was linked to a broader approach to selling cars: less the corporate statement of authority, more an invitation to partnership. This new sophistication of the market is reflected in the provision of massage and aromatherapy alongside natural drinks in the refreshment and relaxation areas.

Partnership not authoritarianism.

The 'Galerie' Ka at Geneva

Dance troupe at the launch of the Puma

client: **Ford of Europe**

fair: **European Motor Shows**

Launching the Puma at Geneva, 1997

As well as presenting a corporate presence, the stand also had to accommodate specific presentations for new models. For the launch of Ka, the car was presented as an individual, informal vehicle, both sophisticated and inexpensive – appealing to the 'young at heart'. The Mondeo theme was understated elegance, style and dynamics, in a serious and professional car. A film for each was commissioned from *Imagination*. The Ka film featured the car moving through a European city by day and night, with a team of dancers communicating the individual personality of the car. The Mondeo film, in contrast, was an abstract black and white A/V compilation, using balletic aerialists in the staged performance. For the presentation of each vehicle, a complete **musical and visual event** was also created. For the Ka, this featured a jazz quartet and a modern tap troupe, while the new Mondeo model was launched by the team of aerialists in white, performing over the vehicle while a light show was projected onto the canopy above. Abstract dance, contemporary music and a specially commissioned film were also used to launch the Puma at the 1997 Geneva Motor Show.

client: **Ford of Europe**

fair: **European Motor Shows**

The color theme was based on the Ford company's proprietary blue, with muted shades of blue used as a background, and natural wood floors and walling on part of the stand, and silvers and grays on others. To support the launch of Ka and Mondeo, press material and client gifts were based around two specially commissioned music selections, one linked to each vehicle, featuring music appropriate to the mood of each vehicle.

The Multimedia Café at Geneva 1997

Video display for the new Mondeo

The design task therefore operated on two levels. One was to evolve a design for the stand which could be used as a common structure for other shows in Europe. The other was to create a particular environment for the new models presented in Birmingham, Paris and Geneva, and which could be grafted seamlessly onto the main stand. At the same time, the stand structure would have to develop to accommodate other presentations in the future.

client: **Ford of Europe**

fair: **European Motor Shows**

'Edge architecture' at Geneva

Imagination's approach showed both creativity and immense professionalism. It was the result of a long and deep understanding of the client, and of the wide range of skills available within a mature, world-class design firm.

1 Starting Out

A trade fair stand is not just a showcase for a company's goods or services, but acts also as a meeting point. This is true whether the fair is a public or professional one, and, if the latter, whether there is a regular schedule of meetings or just a 'drop-in' arrangement for passing visitors. So the first task for any designer is to provide both meeting space and display space. The four projects in this first section look at how these problems can be solved in fairly small spaces, both in aisle and island layouts. (An aisle stand has only one side open to the public, being set against a wall: an island stand is a free-standing one, accessible, if need be, from all sides.)

Vero & Didou are a small French lighting company who started out in stage design. Their stand at the major Paris Lighting show was something of a transformation scene, turning the exhibitor's shell system into a dramatic setting for their new designs.

In designing a stand for Azur, a water environmental company, *Powerhouse Exhibits* in San Diego had a double brief – to create an island stand that could be reconfigured as an aisle stand. Their solution was metaphorical and imaginative: Azur is mainly a service company, so large displays of equipment could give place to meeting areas against an attractive background.

For Emašport in Zagreb, Croatia, *Perfectum Expo Team* had to show two product ranges from major sports manufacturers equally distributed by the client. Their solution also provided the right mix of display, enquiry areas and meeting facilities.

Hoxan supply wall and floor covering material to the Japanese market. Since they produce both modern and traditional designs, their stand at a major professional fair in Tokyo needed to symbolize these jointly, whilst creating identifiable areas for each product range.

What all these projects show is that small scale does not have to restrict the designer's imagination, or stop less being more.

client: Vero & Didou, Clamart, France
designer: In-house design team
product/service: Contemporary lighting design
fair: Salon International de la Lumière, Paris
date: January, 1996

In making the best of a very small space, *Vero & Didou*, a young team of French lighting designers presented their first collection at the major French lighting fair, SIL (Salon International de la Lumière), which is held every two years in conjunction with the main furniture fair, the Salon du Meuble.

client: **Vero & Didou**

fair: **Salon International de la Lumière**

stand size: **Aisle stand, 12.5 square meters (41 square feet)**

total production time: **3 days**

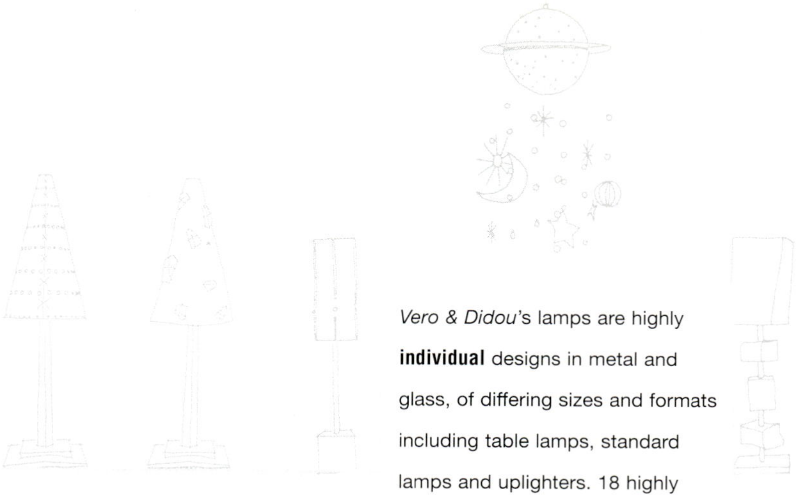

VERO & DIDOU

Vero & Didou's lamps are highly **individual** designs in metal and glass, of differing sizes and formats including table lamps, standard lamps and uplighters. 18 highly individual lamps needed to be displayed within a very **tight space**, and to an even tighter budget.

General view of the stand

client: **Vero & Didou**

fair: **Salon International de la Lumière**

Devising a design solution for a range of objects, each with their own personality, in a small space is very demanding. The space also had to have a table for meetings, and smaller tables to display some lamps in the round. The stand space offered by the exhibition organizers was an open five meter box with side walls of two and a half meters (16.5ft x 8ft). *Vero & Didou*'s solution was to break up the back wall with four panels each two meters high (6.5ft), set at angles to each other to break up the space. In each panel, frames with supporting shelving were cut to display individual lamps. The frames were edged with cardboard surrounds painted silver (the base color for the panels was an off-white). The frames were backed with cloth stapled to the rigid edges, both to reduce weight and offer a difference of texture.

client: **Vero & Didou**

fair: **Salon International de la Lumière**

The tables were made from scrap construction tubing in heavy cardboard, with fitted wooden lids, also painted off-white. The meeting table was a larger tube, with an overhanging circular top. This was reinforced with wooden battens for strength, and an exposed shelf was built on the inner side to provide storage for catalogs and documents.

Informality accentuates product individuality.

Plan (above) and construction details for stand furniture

This deliberately laid-back approach to designing the stand meant that it reinforced the individuality of the lamp designs, a touch accentuated by the slightly crazy angles for the frames. The four-part screen also concealed the switch boxes and wiring, a necessary but disfiguring element in a stand design for a lighting show.

This design shows how a **successful low-cost** stand can be created from basic materials, given an understanding of the qualities of the products to be displayed. Touches such as the silver-painted card frames and the garden chairs add to the quiddity of this excellent project. That *Vero & Didou* come from a background in theatrical lighting and stage design is clear from the subtle *mise en scène* of the stand.

Three of the lamps designed and produced by *Vero & Didou*

client: Azur Environmental, CA. 92008, USA

designer: Powerhouse Exhibits, San Diego, CA., USA

product/service: Water purification

fair: WEFTEC '96, Water Environment Federation, 69th Annual Conference & Exposition, Dallas, Texas, USA

date: October 5th–9th 1996

Azur Environmental, specialists in environmental testing systems for the water industry, needed a small stand for conference-style meetings and product presentations at invitational trade events. They wanted an island stand for the first showing, but asked Rob Quisenberry of *Powerhouse Exhibits* in San Diego to create something for them that could also be reconfigured as an aisle stand.

client: **Azur Environmental**

fair: **WEFTEC '96**

stand size: **122 square meters (400 square foot)**
convertible island stand
total production time: **September 7th–27th 1996**

AZUR ENVIRONMENTAL

The design of an **island stand** – one which can be accessed from all four sides – poses a particular problem, in that while there may be a main access, someone approaching the stand from the other side or sides needs to be able to recognize it, and to feel welcome. *Powerhouse Exhibits* solved this by placing the main structure of the stand **across the diagonal**, in the form of a series of arches. The 'main' access was fronted by a receptionist's desk, while the central block was surmounted by the Azur logo which is echoed on the other side and supported there by display lightboxes.

Using the angle on a square stand to maximize impact on the floor.

Presentation sketches used in client meetings

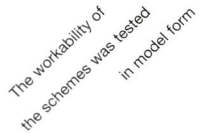

The workability of the schemes was tested in model form

client: **Azur Environmental**

fair: **WEFTEC '96**

'We chose the idea of a jungle temple as a metaphor for the environmental probity of Azur.' Rob Quisenberry.

The principal access, with imitation waterfall behind the reception desk

The design motif for the stand was an imitation Mayan ruin, with an artificial waterfall under the main logo, and plant boxes on the upper edges, underscoring the client company's environmental activities. The fake waterfall made the specific link to the company's water testing systems, in which it is a world leader. This design was developed through models and drawings, and in discussion with the client. The elements can also be reused to create an aisle stand on a 61 square meter (200 square foot) platform.

The central metaphor of the stand is not only a link to Azur's professional activities in the environmental field – their Microtox system is widely used to check water supplies for micro-organisms and toxins – it is also visually refreshing and exciting, and a deliberate contrast to the more formal presentations typical of other stands in a professional show. It uses the language of a public show in a narrower context, so generating a broader appeal. This was also a factor in designing a stand that could be reused in other contexts and configurations.

Workstation and storage areas behind the transversal façade

29

client: **Azur Environmental**

fair: **WEFTEC '96**

Powerhouse Exhibits are specialist exhibition stand designers and builders who take a stand project through from concept to installation. Their work has received several awards, including one for 'Best Idea Never Produced'. Their work features a vivid visual imagination combined with a careful use of materials and strong attention to finish and appearance.

The elements reconfigured as an aisle stand

client: Emašport, Zagreb, Croatia
designer: Perfectum Expo Team, Zagreb, Croatia
product/service: Sportswear
fair: Sportswear Fair: Sports Show '96, Zagreb
date: 1996

King Solomon's radical solution to sharing something is well known. Such a difficult decision can also be put to a stand designer – but luckily the objects in question are inanimate. Emašport distribute two main sports brands in the Croatian market. How then, to show them both equally on the same stand?

client: **Emašport**

fair: **Sports Show '96, Zagreb**

stand size: **130 square meter (425 square feet) aisle stand**
total production time: **1 month**

EMAŠPORT

Emašport represents both Reebok and Umbro. While Reebok specialize in shoes, and Umbro in sportswear, both are in the sports/leisure clothing market as well. Separate small stands for them at the main Croatian sports fair would have been logistically complex for the stand personnel, and would reduce the impact of Emašport's own identity. The *Perfectum* design group in Zagreb were invited to solve this **space-sharing** problem.

'Creating equal space for competing product lines, each with a strong identity.'

Their solution was to **divide** the stand into two halves from the back wall forwards, and use one half for each brand. The layouts of each half mirrored the other, but visitors could pass from one side to the other. Along the central line there was a video booth with a large-screen TV facing onto the front aisle; then the wardrobe and kitchen areas. At the back of the stand there were two closed meeting areas, each with two tables. Around the exterior sides of the meeting areas, so facing both onto the side aisles and the interior of the stand, were display cases for products. Similar **'shop windows'** were placed facing onto the stands on the outside of the wardrobe and video booth. There were separate but matching curved reception desks in front of each meeting room.

The video unit provided both an invitation to passers-by, and formed a divider for the two halves of the stand

client: **Emašport**

fair: **Sports Show '96, Zagreb**

The hall has a low ceiling and poor lighting, so creating a well-lit interior under a suspended ceiling drew visitors into the space

To highlight the three identities, *Perfectum* designed angled towers that projected over the outer corners of the stand, one for Umbro, one for Reebok. Emašport's own logo and corporate color was incorporated into a band above the video booth, and onto the fascia of the suspended ceiling over the core of the stand. This enclosed area had the feel of a sports shop, so the showcases were glazed floor to ceiling to resemble shop-windows.

The flying buttress pillars – each carrying one of the brand names – concealed the supporting columns of the hall which would otherwise have disfigured the stand

33

client: **Emašport**

fair: **Sports Show '96, Zagreb**

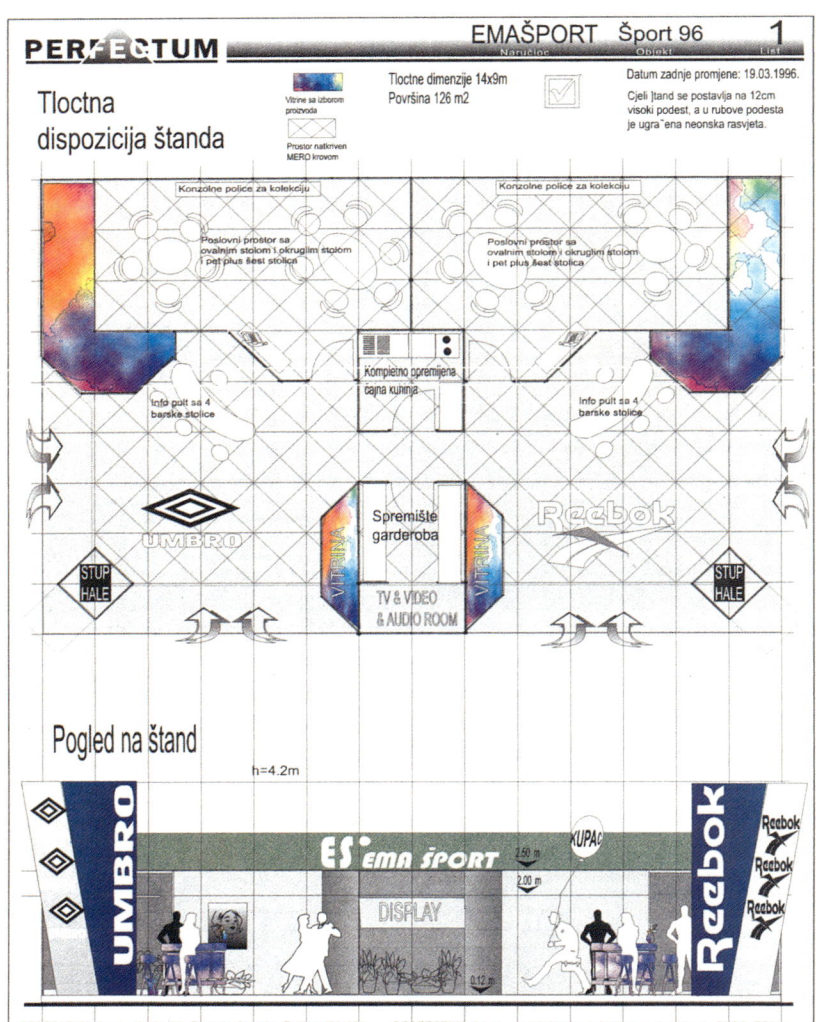

This plan shows the disposition of elements and potential patterns of visitor flow

On the elevation, note the use of abstract human figures to animate the proposal.

Perfectum used the Meroform construction system, which is based on an anodized aluminum frame with white filler panels, for this stand. As Dejan Cehlic, the production manager, points out, this solution was rapid and inexpensive, as all the material was rented. It provided a functional interior space which put the accent on the professional business conducted at the fair.

Perfectum have created over 400 exhibition stands for shows in Germany, Italy, Austria, Hungary and Russia, as well as in Croatia. They have won a number of awards for their work, and specialize in the creation of simple but effective small stands in this growing local market.

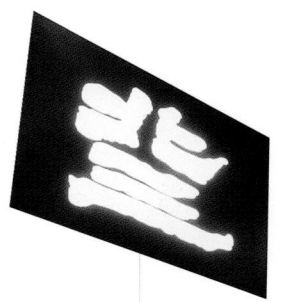

client: Hoxan Co., Tokyo, Japan

designer: MIK Planning Inc., Tokyo, Japan

product/service: Floor and wall covering material

fair: Architect & Construction Materials Show, Harumi, Tokyo, Japan

date: March 1995

Hoxan produce floor and wall covering materials, mainly for the Japanese market, using both conventional materials and new ones, and so, adaptable to both traditional and modern interiors. For the 1993 Japan Shop exhibition Kunio Ogawa and his colleagues at *MIK Planning Inc.* had produced a forest of columns with high exterior walls. When it came to the 1995 Architect & Construction Materials Show, another mainly professional event but with the emphasis moved from the retail environment to architectural spaces of all kinds, Ogawa decided to explore the theme of exterior/interior in a new way.

client: **Hoxan Co.**

fair: **Architect & Construction**

stand size: **Single-level island stand, 216 square meters (12 x 18 meters) (40ft x 60ft)**

total production time: **2 months concept through to completion**

materials: **Floor – needle punch carpet and 'ekki' wooden slate/wall covering – wallpaper**

HOXAN

The stand was on a 12 x 18 meter (40ft x 60ft) platform, and the initial concept was to mask the stand with an angled wall, which would serve as formal entrance and invitation. Through an opening in the wall there would be a bridge, built to a **traditional** design with 'ekki' wooden slats.

An early perspective project shows the bridge turning the stand into an island, with a garden area limiting it, and a display wall behind. 'This technique,' Ogawa explains, 'of going through the wall surface was used in order to differentiate totally the impression of **outside and inside**.'

An early perspective starts from the metaphor of bridge and garden, and develops in a conceptual study into a pattern of abstract spaces and forms

client: **Hoxan Co.**

fair: **Architect & Construction**

client: **Hoxan Co.**

fair: **Architect & Construction**

This concept was developed into a more **abstract** project, losing the garden and island motif, and providing more display facilities and meeting areas. Within the space behind the wall, the bridge comes to an end, offering a choice of presentation areas for different categories of materials: conical display cabinets for sample materials on one side, with room-sets showing traditional and Westernized approaches on the other, and a meeting point closing the opposite corner of the stand to the main entrance.

Behind the screen, a range of different areas focus on product groups

Conical display units are surmounted by minimalist black lighting gantries

client: **Hoxan Co.**

fair: **Architect & Construction**

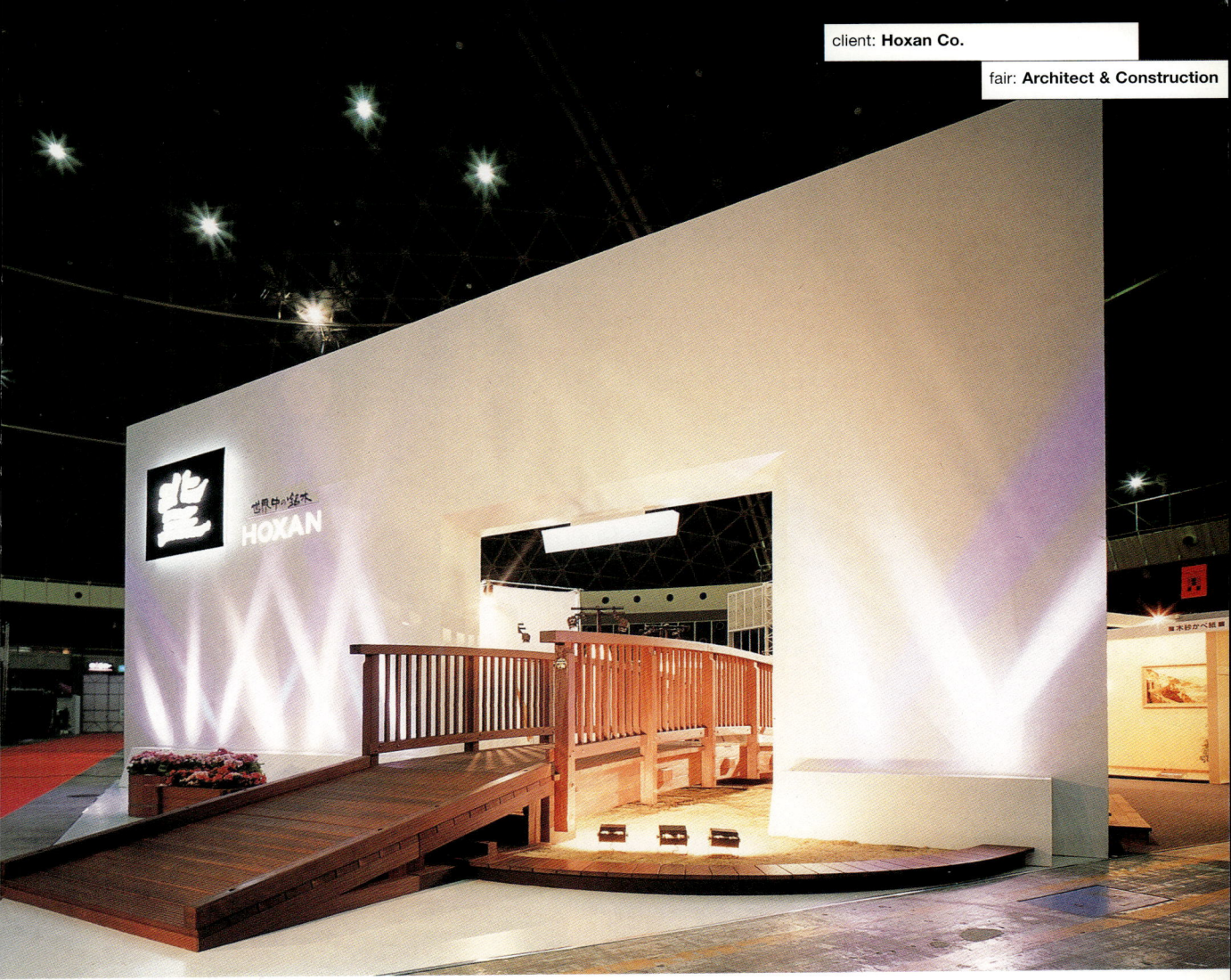

The gentle ramp of the bridge contrasts with the strong six-meter-high (19.5ft) white wall with its dramatic lighting

These areas are differentiated further by the lighting approach: overall lighting was held down to a low level, and supplementary lighting mounted over the display areas. Directional uplighters washing over the exterior wall were also a feature of the stand, animating the surface and hinting at the contrasts within.

Two room-sets contrast traditional and Western styles of decoration

client: **Hoxan Co.**
fair: **Architect & Construction**

client: **Hoxan Co.**

fair: **Architect & Construction**

For the 1993 stand at Japan Shop, *MIK Planning Inc.* chose the denser metaphor of a forest of columns set under a roof at an angle to the floor plan. The two designs, both innovative, show a continuing understanding of the client's approach to the market.

'The concept at the base of this design is the elimination of all decorative elements.' Ogawa.

The 1993 stand

Many stand designs begin as abstract concepts and then develop more decorative metaphors and features. Here the process seems to have happened in reverse. An originally **decorative** plan systematically deleted any decorative elements, except for the 'ekki' bridge, in favor of lighting effects on a mainly white background. The first approach to the stand, confronting the six-meter-high (19.5ft) wall, is extremely expressive, and the choice of a traditional bridge – itself an image replete with **philosophical** and cultural ideas to a Japanese audience – makes a brilliant echo of Hoxan's involvement with both the traditional and the modern.

2 Designing into Space

Joseph Paxton's design for the 1851 Crystal Palace building – the founding parent of all exhibition buildings, which housed the world's first international trade show – was scribbled on a piece of pink blotting paper, then worked into a complete proposal a week later. Jim Martin of *ICON* sketched the design for the main feature of the Trinova Corporation's stand on a paper napkin, and within days had a complete CAD (computer-aided design) model on his computer. So, time-spans for design haven't changed even if the tools have.

This section looks at a group of designs for medium- to large-scale stands which show the design process at work. The Olivetti and Reggiani stands both show how a central idea about presentation and the use of space formulated the whole concept. Mizuno's stand shows how a major event was used to present and organize the working space for the sports goods manufacturer's presentation. For the Philips stand at two successive major electronics shows, the designers used the same central visual concept in different ways to create different and complex environments. For Golden Books Family Entertainment, light and color were the key tools used by the designers to promote a broad marketing message about children's books, while for America OnLine, the very invisibility of the client's product – electronic information – was metamorphosed into a strong visual statement.

Finally, *Root Associate*'s creation of 'Product Heaven' for a computer games expo, shows how rapid visual insight can create a splendid effect from very little material. At the heart of all these projects is the designers' skill in turning visual concepts into a workable professional space, often against tight deadlines or fixed budgetary constraints, and by working closely with the client and gaining a deep understanding of the brief.

client: Olivetti Personal Computers, UK

designer: Can-Can Presentations, London, UK

product/service: Computer hardware

fair: Xana PC launch, Live 96, Olympia, London, UK

date: September 1996

How do you create a surprise within the essentially open and welcoming environment of a trade fair? Some companies do it through a series of presentations, or by walling off part of the stand to create a private theater. For Olivetti, launching a new range of personal PCs at Live 96, the whole stand became the theater.

client: **Olivetti Personal Computers**

fair: **Xana PC launch, Live 96**

stand size: **14m x 12m (46ft x 40ft)**

two-level island stand

total production time: **6 weeks**

OLIVETTI PERSONAL COMPUTERS

Olivetti produced the first commercial typewriter in Italy at the end of the 19th century. Since then the firm has diversified into adding machines, mainframe computers, office furniture and, most recently, desktop and portable PCs. The Olivetti name is also synonymous with discerning design – designers with international reputations such as Ettore Sottsass, Mario Bellini and Michele de Lucchi created this reputation, in part, through their work for Olivetti. In designing personal computers, intensive ergonomic research is matched by a gift for color and form that make Olivetti products distinctive.

The final stand entrance

'Feast your eyes – feed your mind!'

A key problem in stand design is the relationship between inside and outside. What kind of visible partition should mark off the edge of the stand from the surrounding walkways and other stands. Should it be transparent, inviting the passer-by onto the stand by making the goods on show immediately visible, or should it only offer a suggestion or glimpse of what is within (without, of course, turning the curious away). At Live 96 in London, to launch their new range of Xana PCs, Olivetti took this challenge a stage further.

client: **Olivetti Personal Computers**

fair: **Xana PC launch, Live 96**

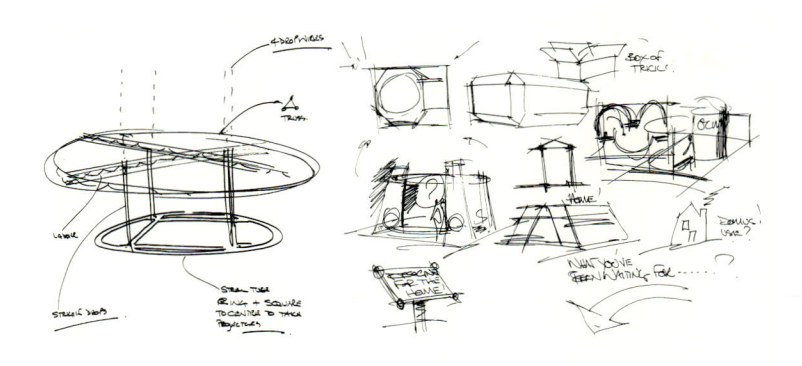

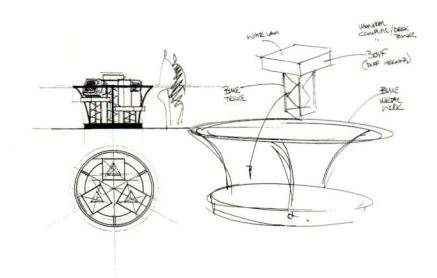

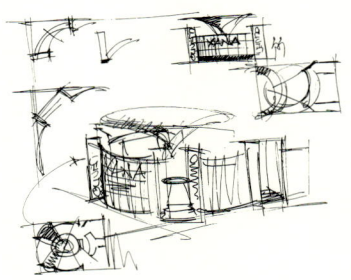

The solution arose also from the nature of the brief. Olivetti was offering a more narrowly-targeted product than some of the other larger exhibitors, and felt that it would reach its market – home users of personal computers for games, multimedia and the Internet – best by individual presentations rather than a free-for-all over the machines on display. Indeed, while providing for a flow-through of 200,000 visitors a day, only four working computers were available.

Sketch designs to develop the curved concept

Color swatches identify the stand colors and materials

Elevation study for the stand frontage

'The show attracts a young audience and the competition is dynamic. We needed to create an inviting experience.' Jenny King, managing director.

client: **Olivetti Personal Computers**

fair: **Xana PC launch, Live 96**

According to Jenny King, managing director of *Can-Can Presentations*: 'We needed an environment that could be informative and fun while being fast and efficient. So, we started by closing off the stand with high walls and restricting access – thereby forcing visitors to enter the stand to discover what was inside. In keeping with the styling of the computer, these walls were curved. Inside, a circular, central viewing area was created. This comprised three front projection video screens each 3m x 2.5m (10ft x 8ft), which gave the audience a sense of panorama. A three-and-a-half minute video module was created to be shown on the screens. This panorama offered us **the opportunity to play** with lighting, video effects and the source and direction of sound.'

Color sketch for the external banner

To support the main presentation, *Can-Can Presentations* also designed a 15m (49ft) promotional banner which adorned the entrance to the exhibition hall, as well as a promotional trailer which was sited on the hall forecourt, and where promotional staff handed out carrier bags to visitors. Olivetti also sponsored a general entertainment area where a live challenge game was played by groups of four competitors at a time. The design concept behind the Olivetti Xana stand is essentially simple. As David to the competitors' Goliath, it had to take advantage of its smaller status by drawing the public in. So, it achieved its success by understanding the psychology of the visitor, by enhancing the visitor's self-esteem and by avoiding a hard sell. Setting up such a change of pace from the general run of marketing-led stands can offer a client a memorable event.

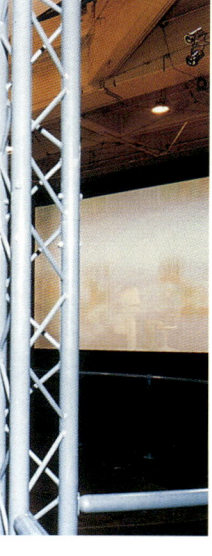

Inside the stand – note the fabric ceiling used for light show projections

client: Philips Consumer Electronics, Knoxville, Tennessee, USA

designer: ICON Incorporated, Fort Wayne, Indiana, USA

product/service: Consumer electronics

fair: Consumer Electronics Show (CES), Las Vegas, USA

date: 1996 and 1997

A company's corporate identity – be it logo, typeface or color – often represents both a major investment by the company and a serious business asset. In designing a trade fair stand the rules of the corporate identity handbook should in principle be respected, unless the brief calls for a different solution (for example, in launching a new product range, when the new name will take precedence).

client: **Philips Consumer Electronics**

fair: **Consumer Electronics Show (CES)**

stand size: **40m x 25.5m (30ft x 84ft) two-decked island stand**

total production time: **3 months**

PHILIPS MAGNAVOX

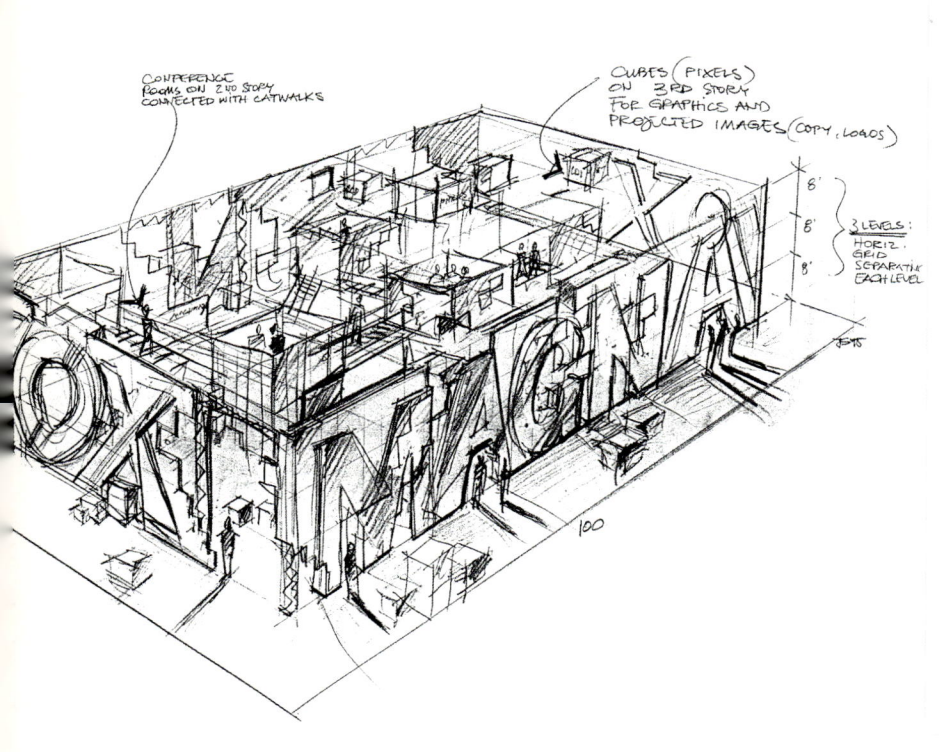

Philips, the giant Dutch electrical company, had mainly developed in the US market by acquiring other companies and retaining their names and brands. However, in recent years they have started to develop the main Philips name. In designing a stand for a major electrical goods fair, the designers at *ICON Incorporated* therefore looked at the ways in which the Philips **chief name** and the brand name, Magnavox, could be strongly presented, together with a suitable visual metaphor for the market position of the company. This process was carried through by a series of meetings with Philips' own exhibition program management group, headed by Lyle Cavanagh.

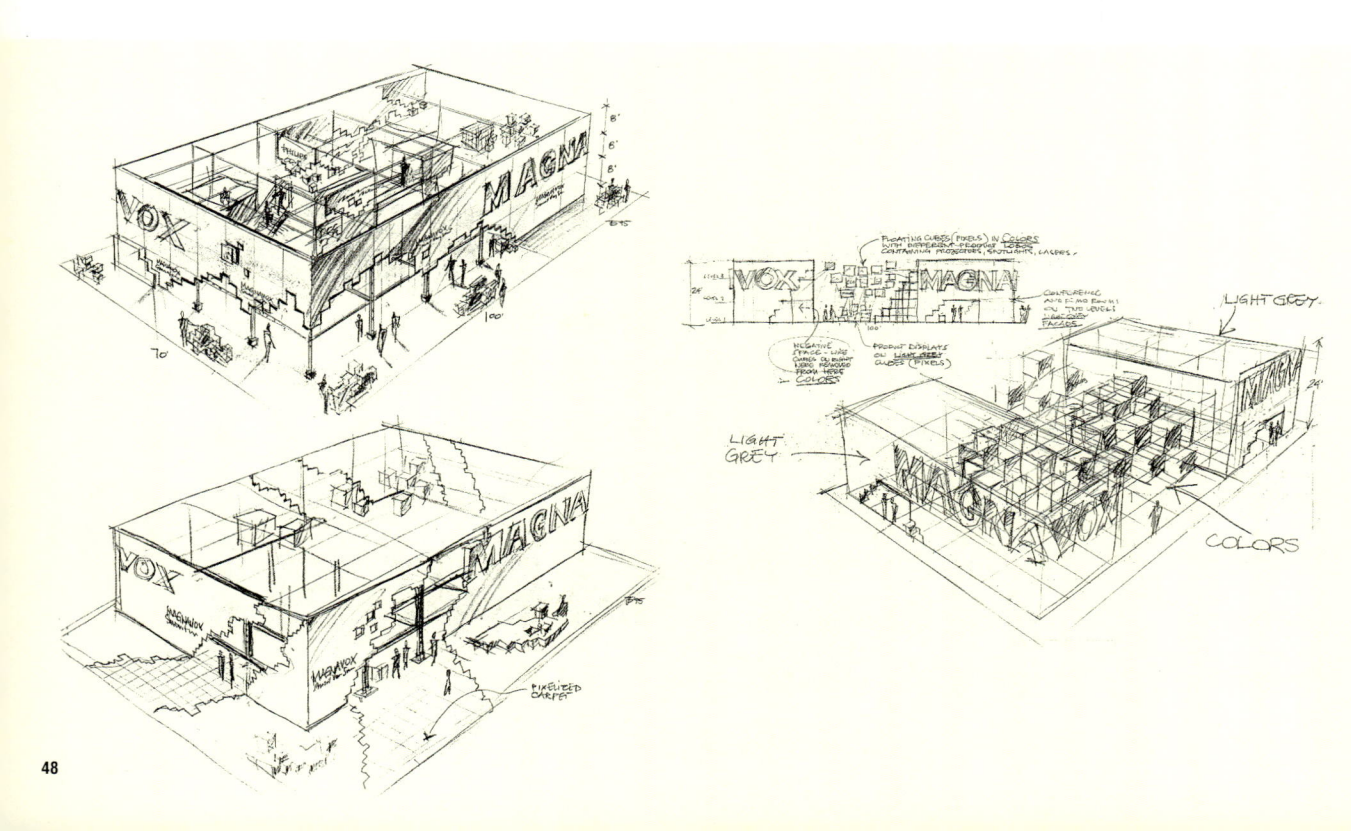

client: **Philips Consumer Electronics**

fair: **Consumer Electronics Show (CES)**

'Philips' commitment to leadership in the digital revolution is the key theme.'
Rich Hostler, Philips.

Different approaches to extending the stand – wall openings in a pixel pattern, or an angled roof – are explored through sketches

One of the best ways to evolve solutions for such a problem is through rapid sketches, sometimes also called scamps, which allow the designer to explore different options rapidly without losing the flow of visual ideas. The different approaches evaluated here, once the basics of the stand size and layout had been decided, are an excellent example of this technique. It was not a matter of thinking onto a blank sheet of paper, however. The brief specified a presentation area to seat 50 people among 15 different activity areas, including portable audio, wide-screen home television, VCRs and new products. Several alternatives were explored to move elements outside the main wall of the stand: for example, an overhead roof canopy set at an angle to the main axis and used for projecting logos and images, and a pair of giant screens, lit from behind hanging cubes, one at each end of the large stand. One metaphor that emerged early for the 1996 CES was '**the box of pixels**' (pixels are the picture cells that are assembled into an onscreen television or monitor image).

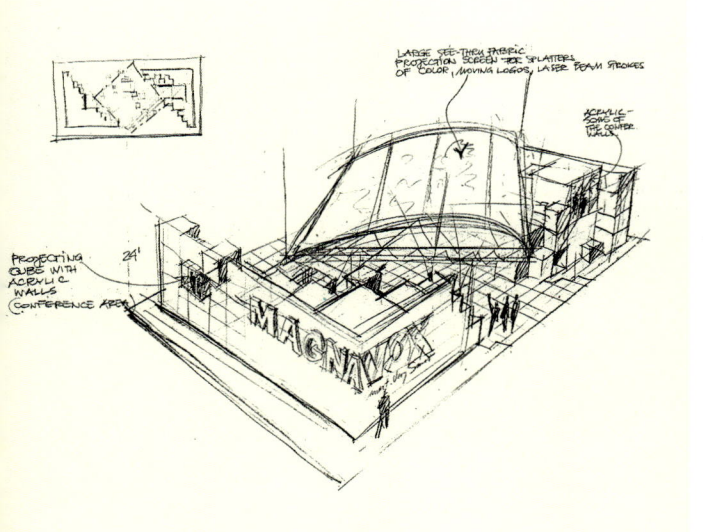

client: **Philips Consumer Electronics**

fair: **Consumer Electronics Show (CES)**

Early concept sketches show the gray exterior walls spelling out the word MAGNAVOX in red, with pixilated entrances, and within the stand, areas marked off by pixilated walls, or floating color pixel-cubes suspended in the air. This concept could also be described as a store interior, and so this metaphor too guided the development of the concept through to finished stand.

Final rendered drawing: note the pixilated effect on the exterior walls

Rendered views of the interior

client: **Philips Consumer Electronics**

fair: **Consumer Electronics Show (CES)**

'Smart Very Smart' (stand strapline for 1996 show).

The 1996 stand complete

From a first range of seven concepts, sketched in black and white, a final version was rendered in color, both the exterior and interior views. These formed the basis for the final plans. Jan Szubiak, the main designer for the 1996 stand, makes the point that **'the client's sensitivity** and sophisticated views regarding contemporary design and architecture – along with a serious budget – presented me with a rare and very fulfilling experience.'

Interior of the 1996 stand

Receptionist's desk at the 1996 stand

51

client: **Philips Consumer Electronics**

fair: **Consumer Electronics Show (CES)**

Despite the fact that the 1996 stand represented a complete break from previous design approaches, client and designer decided that the 1997 show should also present a completely new look. Instead of the rectilinear plan within an outside wall frame used before, the new stand would use a central core on two levels, with flanking, curved display areas outside and within this. The single central theater was divided into two smaller areas, one within the core and one outside, seating 15 people each, and the number of display areas increased from 15 to 19, to make room for new products such as Planet Search and digital cameras.

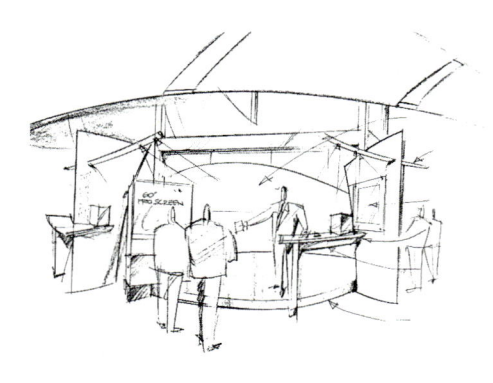

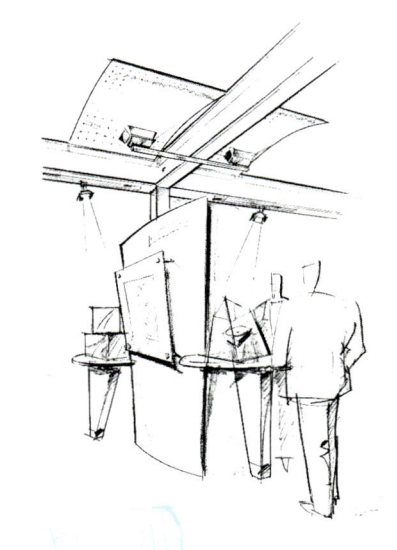

'Let's make things better' (stand strapline for the 1997 show).

Detail studies for furniture, fittings and interiors for the 1997 stand

client: **Philips Consumer Electronics**

fair: **Consumer Electronics Show (CES)**

Rendered drawing of the final design for the 1997 stand

Again, drawings and sketches, both for the overall stand and the details of desk arrangement, presentation areas and monitor stands, were the main route for developing the design. To **build a sense of movement** into the stand, and to break away from the earlier version, curved fabric shapes, some colored, some used as projection screens, were floor-mounted or hung from the ceiling to float above the stand. Thus, while many of the structural elements and displays used at CES 1996 were in fact reused for the 1997 show, the whole visual language of the stand was changed through a comprehensive and extended redesign.

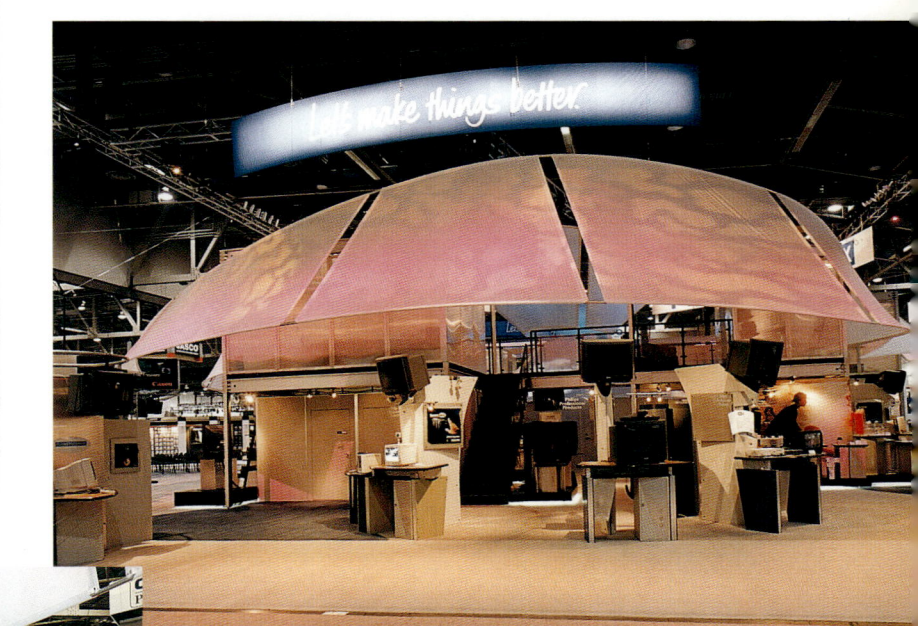

The exterior and interior of the 1997 stand

53

client: **Philips Consumer Electronics**

fair: **Consumer Electronics Show (CES)**

The two Magnavox stands show how teamwork between client and designer can develop concepts rapidly and successfully, and evolve them from show to show. Each project took three months from start to finish, but this needs to be seen against a background of continuous contact and understanding between the partners. The fact that the designs were mainly evolved through sketches is a reflection of this rapid process, but it should not mask the fact that the projects were extremely complex: the main structural plans, the lighting and electronic service plans, the manufacturing specifications for the individual desks and tables, and the logistics documents for construction and assembly were also created within the tight time-span.

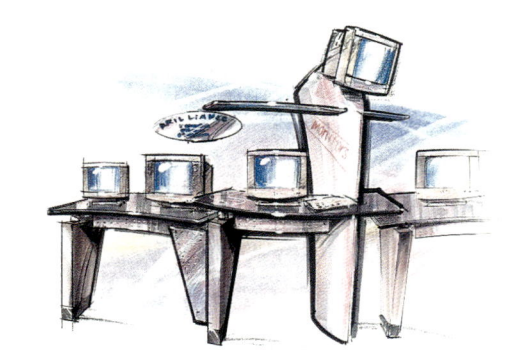

Detail studies in color for the 1997 stand

MIZUNO

client: Mizuno Corporation, Osaka, Japan
designer: Fujiya Co. Ltd., Tokyo, Japan
product/service: General sporting goods manufacturer
fair: Sports Japan, Japan Convention Center, Tiba, Japan
date: 1995

Anyone who thinks baseball is a purely American game should think twice. It has long been popular in the Philippines and in Cuba. There was a summer league in northern England in the 1930s, and the game has been played in Japan for most of the 20th century. It was there in 1906 that Rihachi Mizuno started a small family company to sell baseballs. By the 1930s the firm had branched out into skiing equipment and golf clubs, and today produces a range of sporting goods, sportswear and footwear. With annual sales of over 2 billion dollars, it is the largest general sporting goods manufacturer in the world – and still remains a family-operated business.

client: **Mizuno Corporation**

fair: **Sports Japan**

stand size: **47m x 84m island stand (154ft x 275.5ft)**
total production time: **5 months**

MIZUNO

Sports sponsorship has long been an integral part of the company philosophy: Mizuno sponsored Japan's first Business League Baseball Championship in 1911, and has been involved with the Olympics since 1924. The Mizuno Corporation were official suppliers to the Centennial Olympics in Atlanta in 1996, and their stand at the 1995 Sports Japan exhibition, a major **professional event**, used the Olympics as a theme, under the title 'The World of Sports'.

Sports sponsorship endorses a leading market position.

General view of the fair towards the Mizuno Olympic flame

client: **Mizuno Corporation**

fair: **Sports Japan**

Artist's impression of the 'World of Sports' exhibit

The main entry to the stand was along one of the narrow sides. Here, the main reception area led visitors into a general presentation of tie-in products and retail support, before their being guided to the relevant appointment at one of the 80 or so meeting tables that occupied the main area of the stand. (Such a density of meeting spaces may seem overpowering, but anyone who has worked on such a busy stand will confirm that such a volume of activity actually generates its own **business synergy** and excitement.)

Artist's impression of the main entrance

57

client: **Mizuno Corporation**

fair: **Sports Japan**

The outer edges of the stand became product platforms. An angled framework supported either panels illustrating products and logos, or were fitted with shelves to support life-size figures. The metaphor here was an Olympic podium, with the whole surmounted by the Olympic flame, created in red foam.

The main entrance and logo

The 'World of Sports' exhibit on its raking platform

The Mizuno stand is a statement of corporate authority: notice, for example, the placing of the logo over the entrance area. The use of the exterior shell neatly encapsulates the intense activity within, while making a calm statement of Mizuno's status and prestige, and celebrating their official role in the Centennial Olympic Games.

VICKERS
A TRINOVA Company

client: Vickers Division, Trinova Corporation, Maumee, Ohio, USA

designer: ICON Incorporated, Fort Wayne, Indiana, USA

product/service: Heavy equipment, hydraulic pumps, valves, controls, hoses and fittings

fair: CONEXPO, Las Vegas, USA

date: 1996

Vickers manufacture hydraulic pistons and pumps with a wide range of applications in different mechanical industries. One key use is as power and motion control-units on construction industry equipment, such as excavators and diggers. So if you want to move the crowd, move the earth...

client: **Vickers Division, Trinova Corp.**

fair: **CONEXPO, Las Vegas**

stand size: **Island stand 9m x 12m (30ft x 40ft) with 8m x 4m x 2.5m (27ft x 13ft x 8ft) 'Abstractmobile'**

total production time: **3 months**

TRINOVA VICKERS

ICON Incorporated is a design company, specialists in full-service exhibit design and production, who already worked with Vickers on a number of trade exhibits and presentations. They were approached by Vickers to find a way of showing their new line of hydraulic pistons and ancillary equipment to their own distributors, in the USA and internationally. The first part of the answer was obvious – show the products at work, for example on a twin-shovel mobile excavator. The second part was harder: how to single out the products from the rest of the mechanical 'background' of the excavator digger itself. The answer was to **build your own** one, which is precisely what Jim Martin, the industrial designer, and Mike Bricker, the project manager, set out to do.

The 'Woodie' Abstractmobile on display at Vickers headquarters for the 'Power of Discovery' event

The first idea – on a McDonald's napkin!

client: **Vickers Division, Trinova Corp.**

fair: **CONEXPO, Las Vegas**

The 'Abstractmobile' on the CONEXPO stand

'The result was undoubtedly the best example of a "Just do it!" attitude and execution.' Michael Teadt, Global Communications director, Vickers.

ICON Incorporated first built their excavator digger in unpainted, natural half-inch birchwood-ply. They then built it full-scale and finished, the 'Woodie Abstractmobile' – as it was christened – was 8m (27ft) long and over 4m (13ft) high, standing on four massive wooden wheels. It included not only six of the new Discovery series straight, and T-bar piston pumps, but also 11 other new products, such as vane pumps, brake and truck valves, and manifolds. These key items were clearly visible against the plain background of the natural wood, and indeed were deliberately left exposed. While the model was not fully-functional (as it did not have a power source) the positioning and relationship of the controls, gears and pistons were displayed as they would be on a real machine.

Scale and surface are the key to the project's success: The top of the upper shovel is just over 4m (13ft) from the ground

client: **Vickers Division, Trinova Corp.**
fair: **CONEXPO, Las Vegas**

'Success from a design point of view was due in large part to the few design perimeters set forth by the client.' Jim Martin, industrial designer, *ICON Incorporated*.

Isometric drawings (from the right rear, above, and left front, below) show the 'kit' construction system used

RIGHT REAR ISOMETRIC

LEFT FRONT ISOMETRIC

The **scale** of the design is a key to this **success**. Not only does it show the featured products at full size, but finds a way of presenting them that is immediately engaging. The whole object looks like a childs giant construction kit, a feature emphasized by the open-work wooden plates that frame the assembly. Seeing it looming over the formal heavy engineering tools and gearboxes displayed on adjacent stands must have been like finding a long-lost favorite toy in a forgotten toy-box. The in-house showing was called 'Power of Discovery' a name cleverly and excitingly interpreted by the design team.

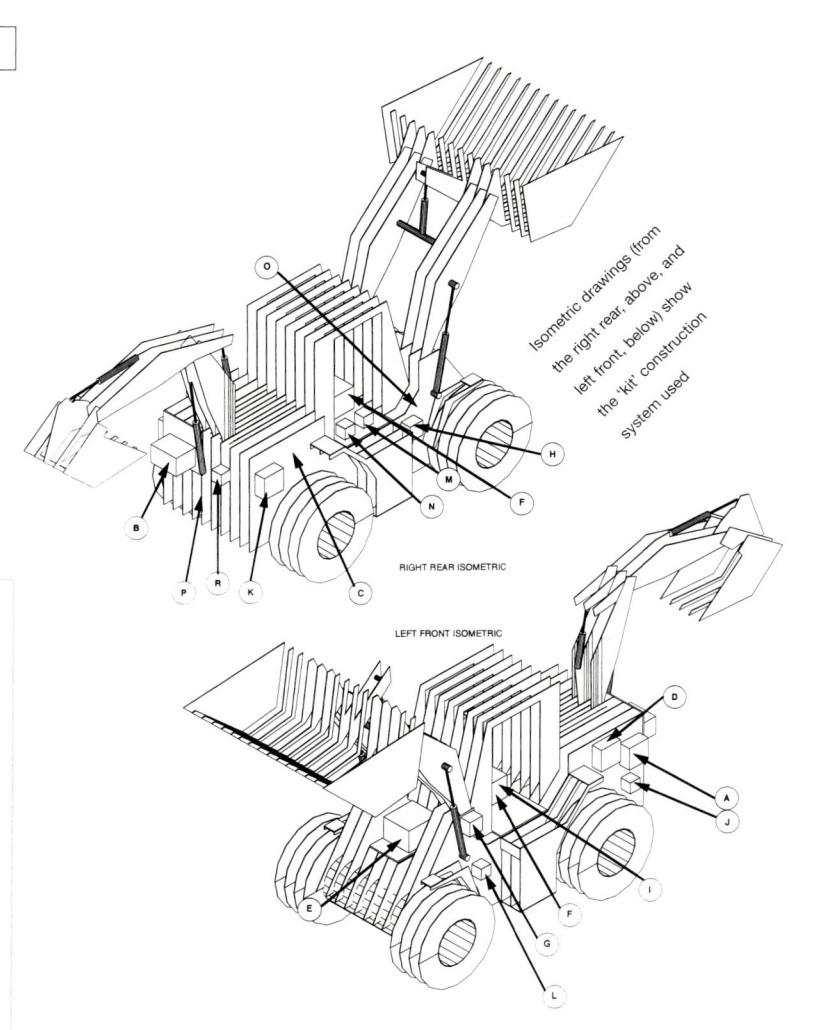

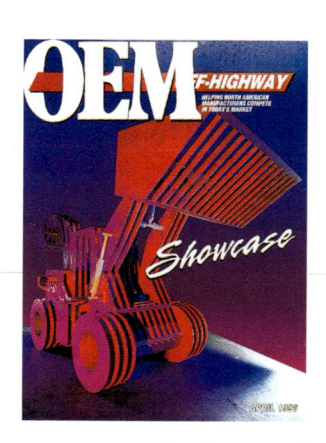

The plain birchwood surfaces provide a neutral background to the fittings

Many who came to the 'Power of Discovery' presentation described it as 'the best industrial event ever attended', and the 'Woodie Abstractmobile' generated similar enthusiasm among the Vickers employees who saw it. By stepping outside the normal vocabulary for presenting technical equipment, and producing instead something both realistic and fantastical, *ICON Incorporated* both met the needs of the client for showcasing a new product range and created an interesting design solution. Not surprisingly, the project received considerable press coverage and won a Design Award.

62

AMERICA Online

client: America OnLine, Dulles, Virginia, USA
designer: Phoenix Presentations, Hamilton, Ohio, USA
product/service: Packaged Online Services
fair: National Association of Broadcasters, Las Vegas, USA
date: April 1996

America OnLine is the largest provider of packaged online services, giving their members access to the Internet and the World Wide Web, together with the use of e-mail and a range of dedicated services ranging from financial information to news stories and travel ideas. The core product, being a service, is in one sense an intangible: what the AOL (America OnLine) member gets is a CD-ROM and a service contract. And the use the members make of the service is defined by them.

client: **America OnLine**

fair: **National Association of Broadcasters**

stand size: **366 square meters (1,200 square feet) two-level island stand**

total production time: **Under 6 months**

AMERICA ONLINE

In planning a new exhibition stand for a major trade event, *Phoenix Presentations* realized that the design had to use the AOL logo as a central motif, as well as invoking the range of opportunities and information the service offers. The pyramid shape echoes the main logo, as do the sweeping 'banners', which also symbolize 'the **communication** of **information** swirling around the pyramid of **power**', according to Carl England, design director. The imagery for the banners was derived from visual elements on AOL's own home page on the Web.

Under the general umbrella of signing the stand with the AOL logo, the brief called for a number of specific spaces and elements. Firstly, there had to be a theater area for public presentations; secondly, a number of demonstration areas for individual 'hands-on' investigation (the demo station counters use the metaphor of surfing the Web as a design motif, using hand-applied multi-colored vinyl to mimic the look and feel of a surfboard); thirdly, an e-mail access service for members; fourthly, a semi-private conference area; and fifthly, distribution points for give-aways of demo disks (it is standard practice for online service companies to offer free software and an initial free trial period). Around all this there had to be space for technical support and wire management systems, ventilation and general storage.

The pyramid, made from light-weight aluminum tubing, has honeycomb corrugated wall panels which are laminated and attached with Velcro

client: **America OnLine**

fair: **National Association of Broadcasters**

The design process went through three distinct stages. An initial four concepts were presented in sketch form, from which elements were selected by the designers and the client for the final design. The three-dimensional geometry of the swirling banners also required detailed study, through computer and physical modeling. This was organized jointly with Moss engineering who were responsible for fabricating the banners. The largest banner was 45 feet long and was also self-supporting!

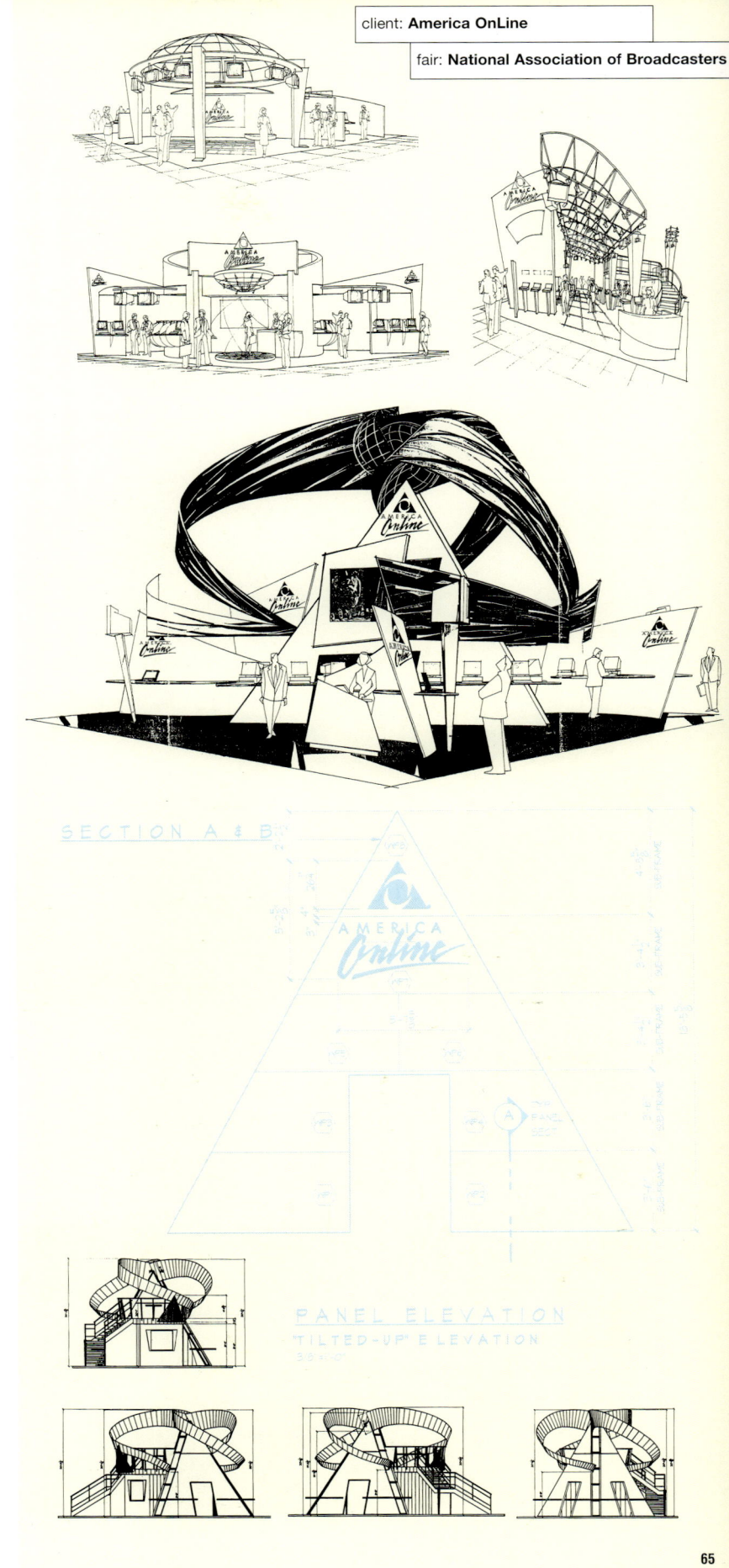

Part of the brief demanded a continuous light show on the exterior, using programed colored lights, gobos and patterns: their design reflects the movement of people within the space and of information through the Internet and Web.

The final stage of the process was the specification and construction. The stand would have to be constructed in a day and a half; it had to be sufficiently light to be transported easily to other locations, and all the processor units and hard drives had to be concealed from the public, though accessible by technical staff.

client: **America OnLine**

fair: **National Association of Broadcasters**

Central pyramid and 27 online systems

Semi-private conference area

Self-supporting banners

3-D computer modeling was used to present the final design to the client

Theater seating

Surfboard countertops

Corner points providing access to give-away material

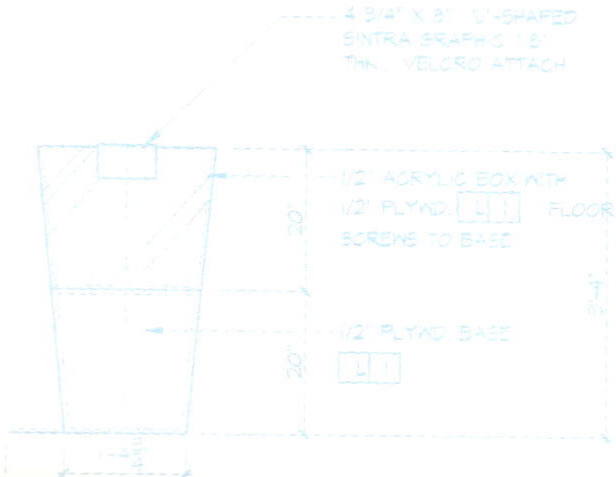

The timing of the design process shows the kind of pressures created by sophisticated trade stand design. The designers' offer was accepted in mid-November 1995, and the final design (and pricing) approved in early January 1996. Final revisions to the constructional drawings, including detail drawings, were complete by mid-February when the proposal went for certification by structural engineers (to ensure it met the fire and safety regulations for the site). Physical production of the design elements began in the last days of February, and the completed stand was shown to the clients at the beginning of April: well under six months in all.

The design consists of a central pyramid, with a presentation theater on one side, and public access points to 27 separate online systems around the base of the pyramid. The swirling banners are self-supporting, and corner points on the site provided access to give-away material.

Phoenix Presentations won an E3 award for the design of the project. They themselves were so proud of their work that they hosted an open house on the site at the exhibition. The stand has been used at five other major trade presentations in the nine months since its first roll-out.

66

REGGIANI

client: Reggiani Spa Illuminazione, Milan, Italy
designer: Toni Zuccheri, Sanvito Al Tagliamento, Italy
product/service: Lighting fixtures
fair: Euroluce, Milan
date: 1996

Reggiani Spa Illuminazione are an established Italian family firm based in Milan and specializing in the design of lighting for commercial and domestic use. They have a strong interest in design, having invited famous international designers to work for them in the past. Milan is the center of the Italian furniture industry, the creative center of contemporary furniture design, and the annual April Salone Del Mobile, the major event in the international calendar. Every two years the Salone is also host to Euroluce, an important event for contemporary lighting design, second only to the annual Hanover Fair.

client: **Reggiani Spa Illuminazione**

fair: **Euroluce**

stand size: **320 square meters (1050 square feet), enclosed aisle stand**

total production time: **5 months**

REGGIANI SPA ILLUMINAZIONE

A fair devoted to lighting poses a certain number of technical problems. One is the management of electrical supply and the other the display of light fittings, since the appearance of the fitting, though important, is only half the matter. The important thing is how well it works: the illumination a fitting creates is the key to its success, not its looks. And a subsidiary problem arising from these is the disposal of the heat generated by the range of lamps and fittings that need to be displayed. Given how warm it can be in Milan in April, the latter is a major headache. For their new range in 1996, Reggiani Spa Illuminazione was presenting three new series of 'lampadaires' – Metamorphosi, Scoop and Sunny Light – two of which were suitable for outdoor or indoor use. The architect *Toni Zuccheri* was invited to **create an environment** to display these.

'Man in relation to water, the sky and light.' Toni Zuccheri.

Often the basic metaphor of a stand is confrontational: visitors on one side, products on the other, as it were. *Zuccheri* wanted to challenge this, suggesting instead a dialog between man (symbolizing thought and dynamics) and the natural elements of water, air and light. He created a series of pools, in rectangular tanks set at a height of 1.10m (3.5ft), through which the visitors moved, and above which the lights were displayed, under a dark ceiling. This was like a cavern of the senses – with reflections of light and color bouncing off water and the ceiling – in a long, narrow and non-cubic space (since the wall along one side was set at an angle). A gentle current of air kept ripples on the water, in turn creating a cooling effect. The resulting space was a complete contrast to the many overlit – and overheated – stands elsewhere at Euroluce. It was, in *Zuccheri*'s words, 'an idea designed and developed to emphasize the primary needs of man in relation to water, the sky and light.' It was an abstract space, **about light** rather than about light fittings, suggesting no specific context for the products other than a human one. This elegant, yet understated presentation, was the main strength of the stand, and made it a memorable one.

client: **Reggiani Spa Illuminazione**

fair: **Euroluce**

General view of stand with 'sky'

client: **Reggiani Spa Illuminazione**

fair: **Euroluce**

The underlying theme of a dialog was also reinforced by the key subsidiary areas of the stand, where Reggiani Spa Illuminazione were launching two related informational products, a CD-ROM version of their lighting catalog, and the Reggiani World Wide Web site, which allows users both direct information download, as well as an Internet link to the company and its branches worldwide.

Using a metaphor to create a mood.

Light effects on the stand

Unlike design practice in some houses in the UK and the USA, where the descriptive vocabulary is taken extensively from business and marketing, in Italy designers and architects are quite happy to draw on **philosophy, semantics, myth and psychology** to validate the design process. Both approaches, if taken to excess, can lead to bathos and even outright comedy, and any serious designer knows that a successful design needs to encompass both a cultural and a commercial element, as well as wit and wisdom. *Zuccheri*'s work for Reggiani shows how the metaphorical approach can be used to present a modern technological product in a direct, non-referential and non-confrontational way.

client: Golden Books Family Entertainment, Wisconsin, USA
designer: Derse Exhibits, Milwaukee, WI, USA
product/service: Children's book publishing
fair: Toy Fair, New York, USA
date: 1995

Golden Books Family Entertainment selected *Derse Exhibits* to design a completely new stand for their children's books from a creative pitch against six other agencies. Winning the brief was only the beginning, however. Kent Jones, vice president/creative for *Derse Exhibits* explains that they were sent on a crash course on the company. 'They drove us all over the countryside, taking us to different booksellers, doing research, educating us about who they were and who they wanted to be. It was tremendous.'

client: **Golden Books Family Entertainment**

fair: **Toy Fair, New York**

stand size: **1067 square meters (3,500 square feet) independent stand**

total production time: **6 months**

GOLDEN BOOKS

The site for the stand was along a wall some 24.40m long (80ft), accessed to by a lobby entrance at one end, which led through into the exhibition area on one side, and a suite of conference and meeting rooms on the other. In the lobby area there would be a short video, written and produced by *Derse Exhibits*, setting out the company and its imprints through the use of images of children reading. 'Golden Books Family Entertainment have a strong product focus and **a clear family-oriented marketing message**.' Kent Jones explains, 'and we wanted to create an ambience that engulfed you in the Golden Books experience. The goal was to make people feel that Golden books were about family values.'

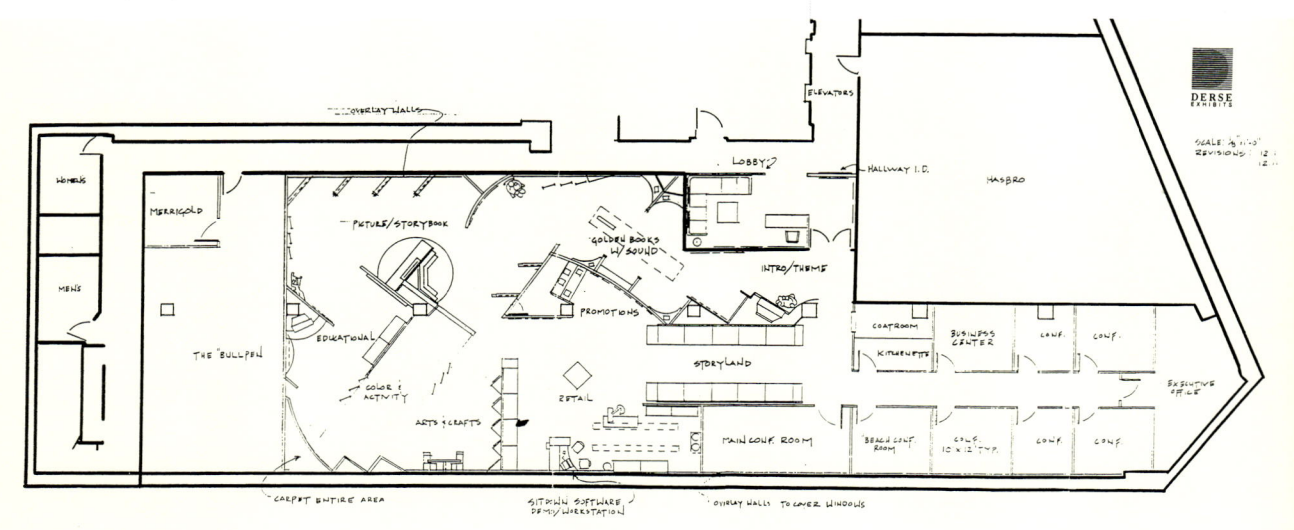

Plan of the stand showing exhibition area, foyer and meeting rooms

Entrance to the stand

'We wanted people to feel that Golden Books were about reading, learning and the family.'

The initial sketches show how this was to be achieved through dividing the stand into strongly-colored areas, with highly directional lighting. With dark carpets and ceiling, the idea was to generate through a main color, a **mood specific** to each area: story books to be read aloud, craft and activity books, and tie-in titles, for example. By using positive lighting, the color lets the books jump off the walls as well.

client: **Golden Books Family Entertainment**

fair: **Toy Fair, New York**

In the final execution the low ceiling is used to mount tracked spotlights which create the lighting effects, focusing on the walls to heighten the color drama. These colors have also been strengthened in comparison to the sketches, showing how the values of the original idea were developed in the final execution.

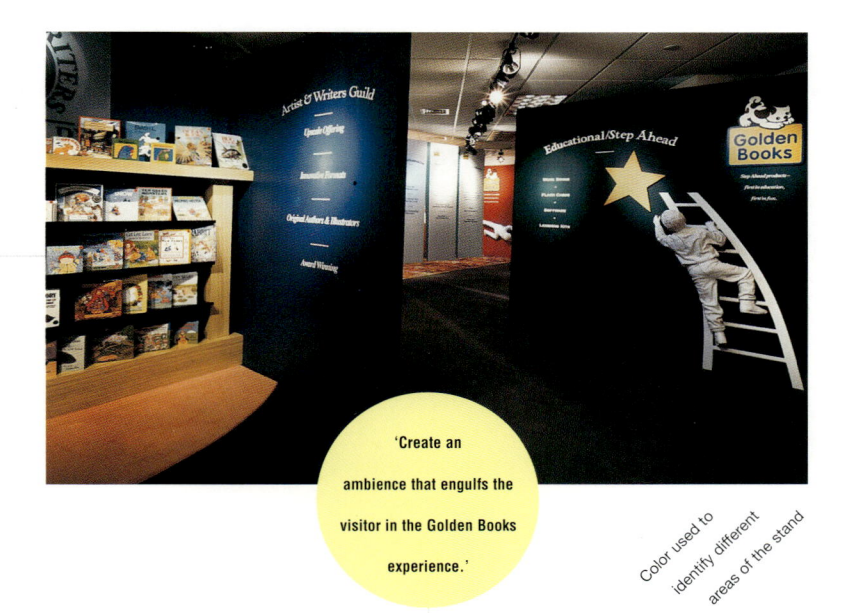

'Create an ambience that engulfs the visitor in the Golden Books experience.'

Color used to identify different areas of the stand

Another feature developed was a series of white, life-size sculptures of children, parents, friends and grandparents reading. One figure or group is used to identify each area, and rather than posing them simply on the floor, some, such as a boy lying down reading, were attached to the walls. These bring a dimension that is both abstract and human (the figures are reminiscent of the 1960s sculptures of George Segal), and underscore the marketing message, that reading is a natural and good family activity.

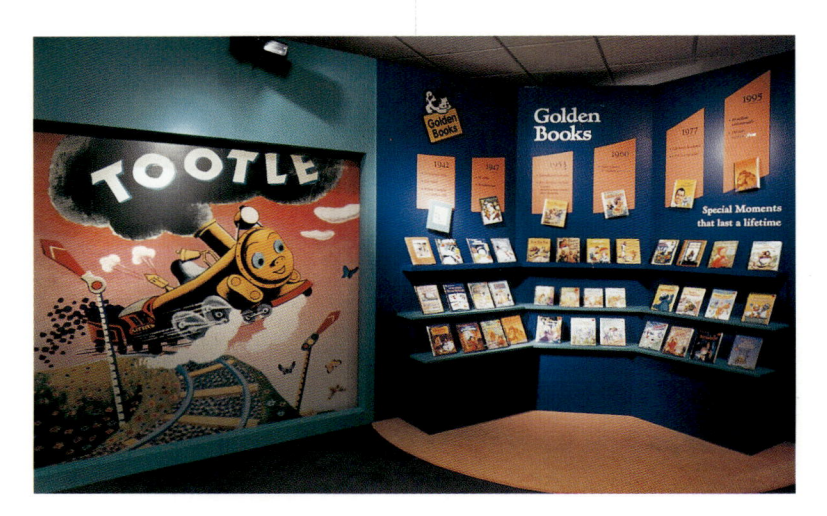

Visualizations of the stand interior for client presentations

Spotlighting used to highlight product sections

73

client: **Golden Books Family Entertainment**

fair: **Toy Fair, New York**

While the exhibition space is relatively small for the **density of imagery, color and light**, it should be borne in mind that Toy Fair is a professional exhibition and visits to the stand were by appointment only. Thus, visitors to the stand had the time and space to savor its contents.

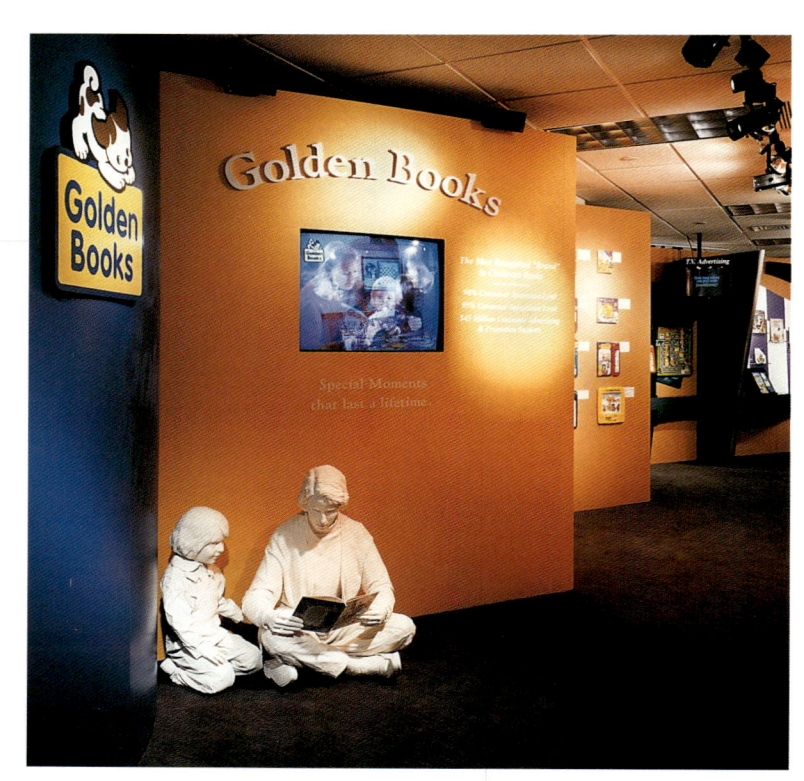

Sculpture and video unit integrated into the 'reading aloud' section

Books for young readers: the floor is made up from laminated book covers, while the sculpture of the reading child is set on the end wall

Golden Books Family Entertainment were looking to strengthen their marketing position via the Toy Fair presentation, without losing the support of core customers. The training program for the design team – the investigation and explanation of the company that preceded the actual design phase – paid off in a very successful fair and a Design Award for *Derse Exhibits*.

product | heaven

client: GT Interactive, London, UK
designer: Root Associates, London, UK
product/service: Computer games
fair: Electronic Computer Trade Show, Olympia, London, UK
date: March 1995

One of the key challenges for a fair exhibitor is how to create private space and quality time for professional visitors. While the bustle of the aisles contributes to the vigor of a fair, it can also cause distractions for meetings and presentations on the stands themselves. GT Interactive, a major player in the computer game field, felt that they wanted to create a special experience for their visitors to a professional trade fair in London. They approached the London-based design agency *Root Associates* for help.

client: **GT Interactive**

fair: **Electronic Computer Trade Show**

stand size: **Enclosed stand within presentation suite**

total production time: **2 months**

GT INTERACTIVE

Developing a logo based on the idea of angel's wings and helping hands

Because the budget was very restricted, the designers aimed to create a new area within the existing suite of offices at Olympia where GT were meeting clients, and for the design motif, hit on the idea of '**Product Heaven**' – out there in the aisles it was hell, but here it would be heaven!

The concept of heaven needed visual expression, so the designers brainstormed the idea through drawings. **Angels and cherubs**, haloes and stained glass, fluffy white clouds and outstretched wings, and the eye of god: all these were sketched out to provide a starting point for the design which had to be completed and installed in under two months.

client: **GT Interactive**

fair: **Electronic Computer Trade Show**

Brainstorming visual ideas as the first step in the design process.

The key elements retained were stained glass, haloes and cherubs. Stained glass was to be used to set the scene by the entrance to the area, with a golden cherub next in line, presiding over the entry to the product area.

A welcoming cherub...

...and stained-glass windows set the scene

77

client: **GT Interactive**
fair: **Electronic Computer Trade Show**

In the main area, consoles and monitors for the games were placed on white stands and surmounted by neon lamp haloes. The whole interior was draped in soft white muslin in order to emulate **the interior of a cloud**. In the center, a rotating, faceted silver ball spins, surrounded by the open, working title 'Product Heaven'.

The interior of 'Product Heaven' is seen here, complete with haloes

client: **GT Interactive**

fair: **Electronic Computer Trade Show**

The central light-ball with the name and logo

Getting away from the fair to a product heaven was the key to the brief.

This design does not aim to make a grand statement: it has a deliberately light touch. Notes on the design drawings, for example, suggest 'kitsch memorabilia' as a theme. But the design also provides an uncluttered and unusual space in which the products can be presented, and which will stick in the visitor's mind, through its originality, long after more elaborate stands have been forgotten.

Root Associates were able to achieve this remarkable and economic design through strong graphic skills, through a clear understanding of what the client needed, and through working closely with the constructors, Heavy Pencil. In its rapid evolution, and simple execution, 'Product Heaven' is an excellent example of design creativity at work within a brief.

3 Presenting the Client

Major national and international trade fairs are large and getting larger – larger numbers of visitors, larger numbers of exhibitors, larger stands and larger budgets. Thus, one of the main challenges faced by the designer is not simply to maintain the client's visibility, but to make the stand into a compelling corporate statement. This design aspect also has to fit seamlessly into the professional requirements of the stand: the number of visitors, the number of products to be displayed, the nature of any special presentations or theater events, the division between public areas and private meeting spaces, and so forth.

Often the design brief will go beyond merely designing the stand into creating supplementary material – videos and leaflets, press packs and presentations. Many stands make use of contemporary presentation technologies using wide-screen television screens with presenters and even actors. The stands in this section bring together not only the creative skills of the design team, but also organizational and planning talents, and other design skills in writing scripts for presentations, and producing and directing video material. This requires close cooperation with the client, and a strong comprehension of the client's requirements and the opportunities provided by the event.

The Microsoft stand, for example, has seven or eight simultaneous presentations running at any one time, as well as a range of games consoles. The electrical supply and computer maintenance problems required by this alone are similar to the needs of a small office building. The Intel stand had to be designed so that it could be dismantled and rebuilt a dozen times over a two-year period, together with a complex multimedia presentation within the stand. For Mercedes-Benz, apart from the dynamics of the stand itself, there was the continuous link to an outside site to develop and maintain. And for Ericsson and Virgin Interactive there were teams of actors and presenters to be trained. These mature examples of expo design require not only design ability, but design management and teamwork.

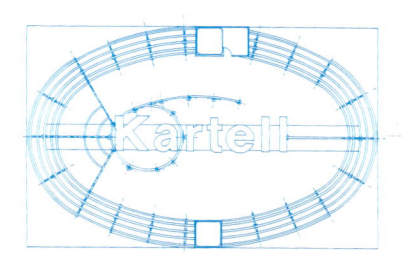

client: Kartell S.p.A., Milan, Italy

designer: Pietro-Ferruccio Laviani

product/service: Furniture design

fair: Salone del Mobile, Milan, Italy

date: 1993–1996

The Milan Salone del Mobile is the central event in the contemporary furniture fair calendar, and Kartell, who have a regular position at an island stand on the first floor of the main contemporary furniture hall, are major players in the field. Investment in their stand design each year is a clear marketing commitment.

client: **Kartell S.p.A.**

fair: **Salone del Mobile, Milan, Italy**

stand size: **Single-level island stand**

total production time: **Continuous redesign**

KARTELL

For the designer working in such a competitive field, almost every approach to displaying furniture has been tried already. The parameters of the design in Kartell's case were also important. Their stand is one of the most visited ones on the fair, so free and rapid access was a necessity. At the same time, key visitors – international buyers, journalists and designers – had to be identified, met and welcomed. And the furniture had to be seen.

The 1993 stand

client: **Kartell S.p.A.**

fair: **Salone del Mobile, Milan, Italy**

In 1993 the architect *Pietro-Ferruccio Laviani* took on responsibility for what had always been one of the most exciting stands at the Salone. At the same time, Kartell, under the new proprietorship of Claudio Luti, was launching a new range of furniture using plastics, including the highly-successful range presided over by French designer Philippe Starck. For *Laviani*: 'in my view the important thing is not just to work around the end product, but to follow lines of research around the brief – into design tendencies, into color preferences, into materials and finishes, keeping alert to the cultural events that are the agents of change in taste. For Kartell production is polyglot. It is aimed at various markets, and adapts to different categories of choice.'

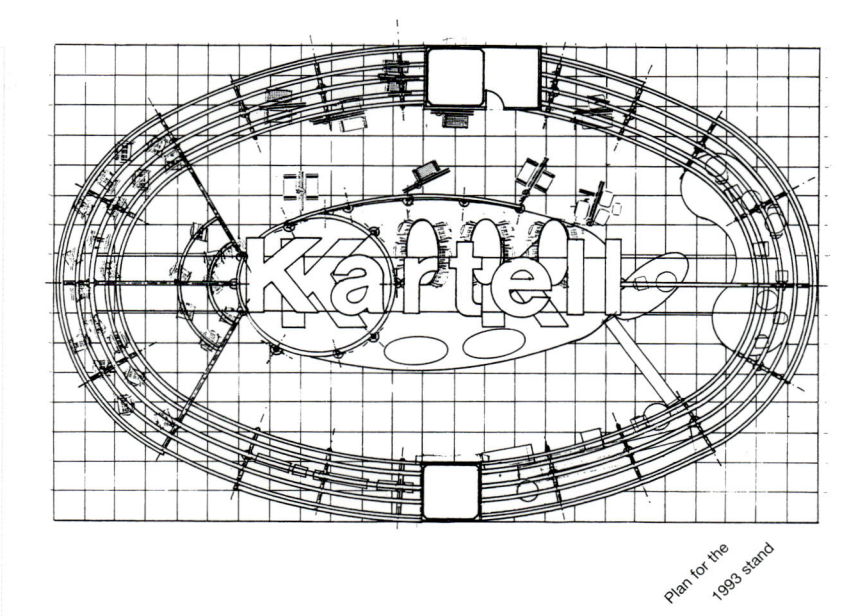

Plan for the 1993 stand

For Kartell, production is multilingual: it has to work in different markets and styles.

Laviani's successive designs for the Kartell stand between 1993 and today act as a mirror both of the evolution of the Kartell product range and of design taste. Each year has witnessed a different but subtly related **design metaphor for the presentation**. This intelligent, highly visual and almost lyrical approach to design is wholly appropriate to Kartell, a company where design values are embedded in the corporate culture, as well as being a key aspect of the final product.

In 1993 *Laviani* created a swirling cyclotron of a stand, continuously in visual movement. It featured strong orange and blue colors and asymmetrical forms, creating a vortex of activity in the center which drew the visitor in.

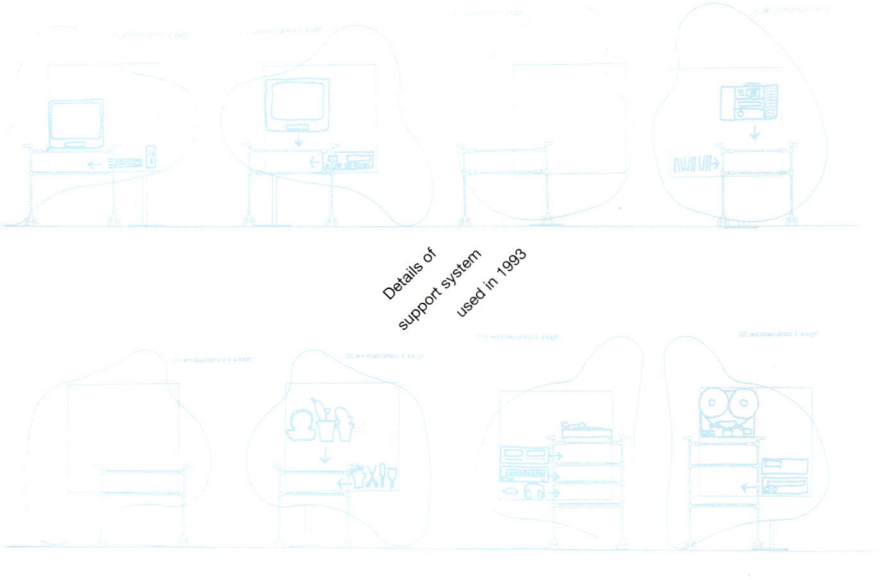

Details of support system used in 1993

client: **Kartell S.p.A.**

fair: **Salone del Mobile, Milan, Italy**

The 1994 stand was a complete contrast. The new furniture was displayed in cool clear columns, lit from beneath with cold white light. This very formal, disciplined solution also echoed a return to order in the market-place, which had been rocked by difficulties of the early 1990s. Yet on closer acquaintance the placing of the columns showed a keen aesthetic sensibility, and the occasional glimpses of strong color made the stand a powerful focus for Kartell's work.

The 1994 stand: the use of under-lighting creates a special atmosphere on the stand

client: **Kartell S.p.A.**

fair: **Salone del Mobile, Milan, Italy**

The 1995 stand

For the 1995 Salone there was another metaphor to hand: Kartell had just published a major new catalog of their work, consolidating three years innovation and growth under the new owner. This, with its clear typography and fine detail in the design, led to a further stand project. This used open red metal-edged boxes standing on thin legs above the floor to display the new work. Like the open pages of a book, in three-dimensional form, these presented the year's chairs, tables and fittings in a quasi-virtual space: unlike the pages of a book, here the visitor can look across, around and behind, seeing the object in a formal yet wholly three-dimensional way.

client: **Kartell S.p.A.**

fair: **Salone del Mobile, Milan, Italy**

Laviani's work for Kartell encapsulates a view of design that sees the company's design policy as an extension of the social and design fabric of everyday life, and a design event, such as a stand or a showroom or a catalog as demonstration and translation of that commitment. Kartell's success as an avant-garde furniture company depends on the customer's total perception of the company, its products, publications and events as meeting absolutely contemporary criteria.

'Using the catalog as a parallel source strengthened the Kartell image.'

Microsoft

client: Microsoft Ltd., Woking, Berkshire, UK
designer: Innervisions Interiors and Exhibitions Ltd., London, UK
product/service: Computer software
fair: Live '96, London
date: November 1996

Live 96 presented computer games, and business and entertainment software and hardware to a broad, and often young, public over a week in London's Olympia exhibition halls. The aim of the fair was to present the product experience direct to potential customers. Microsoft, who had one of the largest stands at the show, divided this market into four main groups: firstly, those interested in office products, particularly the new release of their Office 97 software; secondly, those interested in home-based activities; thirdly, those interested in the Internet (and so, Microsoft Internet Explorer software and the Microsoft Network); and fourthly, those interested in computer games. The overall message to each was that Microsoft products provided the complete business and home computing solution.

client: **Microsoft Ltd.**

fair: **Live '96, London**

stand size: **Two-level island stand, 850 square meters (2790 square feet)**

total production time: **Continuous development program**

MICROSOFT

General view of the stand showing the use of curved motifs

Innervisions is a specialized exhibition design and construction company based in London. They have created a large range of events and exhibitions for Microsoft in the UK and in Europe during the last three years. 'Microsoft are exacting customers,' they explain, 'but there are advantages to a long-standing arrangement which is clearly focused on one activity.' The four categories of visitors identified in the brief each required different treatment. For the games players, hands-on experience was the necessary norm. For those in the home-use category both a demonstration and some hands-on 'test driving' was needed. For Internet and business customers a formal presentation was the appropriate model. The stand was planned around six discrete areas: three presentation units with two presenters, large screens and theater seating, for 'Achieving More at Work with Office 97', 'Fun and Learning At Home', and 'Bring the Internet into Your Home'; two 'test drive' areas ('The Entertainment Zone' and 'Fun and Learning at Home') offering a mixture of **presentations and trials** on monitors; and finally a 'Hot for Windows' games area with 15 individual monitors and joysticks.

client: **Microsoft Ltd.**

fair: **Live '96, London**

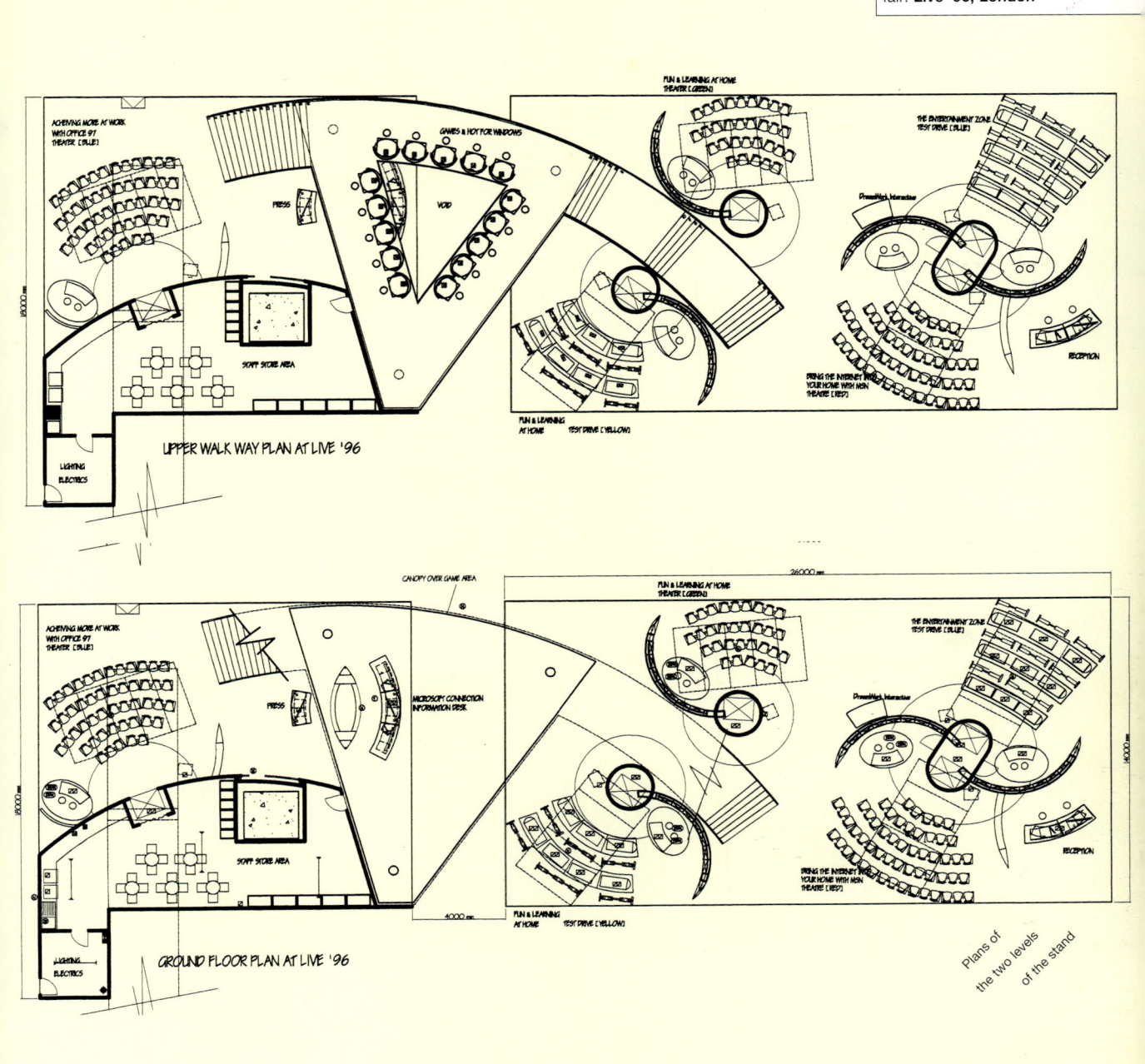

UPPER WALK WAY PLAN AT LIVE '96

GROUND FLOOR PLAN AT LIVE '96

Plans of the two levels of the stand

client: **Microsoft Ltd.**

fair: **Live '96, London**

The upper-level games area forms a bridge between the two parts of the stand

Presenting the product experience.

The games area was on the raised first floor area, reached by sweeping ramps from the ground level area. Each area was color coded for identification. Many of the presentations were **interactive**, featuring actors such as 'The Mad Professor', as well as formal presenters. The configuration of the stand crossed an aisle, with the upper area, in part, over it. There was also a closed area for the staff, lighting and electrical controls. A small press desk and an information desk were also introduced into the design of the stand: the latter gave onto the aisle running through the two halves of the stand.

client:	**Microsoft Ltd.**
fair:	**Live '96, London**

The main design motifs were based around the strong colors selected for the individual areas, the curved screens used to mount the large presentation monitors and the sweeps of the ramps, and the canopy over the games area. These curved structures gave the stand the appearance of a huge, brightly colored and highly energetic turbine about to roar into life. The stand had to accommodate a high flow of visitors – those using the games areas had timed sessions, with hopefuls queuing down the ramps waiting for a turn.

The entrance to the games area – note the effects of lighting and the specially made fittings

client: **Microsoft Ltd.**

fair: **Live '96, London**

The highly independent approach developed here shows through in many details on the stand. Features such as desks and chairs were **specifically designed** and built for Microsoft's own use: even items such as the receptionist's desk had an individual design, unique to Microsoft. This ensures visual and **design coherence**, and no overlap with the design of competitors' stands. The slightly futuristic shape of the chairs, for example, underlines Microsoft's vision of itself as a company enabling the future.

The chairs and tables are specifically created for Microsoft

Mercedes-Benz

client: Mercedes-Benz AG, Stuttgart, Germany
designer: Kauffmann Theilig & Partner, Ostfildern, Germany
product/service: Automobiles
fair: Paris Motor Show, France
date: 1996

The German car makers Mercedes-Benz have worked with *Kauffmann Theilig & Partner* on their stand and event design for a number of years. One major event they created was a 12,000 square meter (39,000 square feet) two-storey stand under a lightweight suspended roof, which was erected in Frankfurt for the Motor Show there in 1995. For the Paris Motor Show in 1996 an equally exciting project was required, though smaller in scale.

client: **Mercedes-Benz**

fair: **Paris Motor Show**

stand type: **1,100 square meters (3600 square feet) two-level island stand**

total production time: **5 months**

MERCEDES-BENZ

The architects' original analysis of the task for Paris, together with the client, was that a stand had a number of functions: press conference, press days, VIP evening events, dealer presentations, and public visitor days. Rather than one stand, ten were perhaps needed. Looking more widely at the underlying marketing proposal for Mercedes, there was, they realized, something of an irony in presenting in static form products that are all about **movement**. So if you couldn't move the cars, then why not move the stand.

Movement is the true state of all things.

Walls could either move or concertina to a new configuration

client: **Mercedes-Benz**

fair: **Paris Motor Show**

General view of the stand exterior with moving wall

The changes to the stand took place continuously

This solution did not mean merely a stand that could be reconfigured, like a stage set, but a stand that would itself move in use, shrouding or unveiling a new model, with walls that would concertina to **reveal** a hidden area, or change to enclose a group of visitors into a new space. The cars were displayed on 15m (49ft) diameter revolving stands, so that they could themselves turn and move during a presentation, or carry visitors to a new area of the stand.

95

client: **Mercedes-Benz**

fair: **Paris Motor Show**

The concept of an **evolving** stand with space and atmosphere underpins and develops the basic communication themes: that movement is the state of things. The physical design was for a series of moveable wall units constructed on birchwood frames on a 50cm x 50cm (1.6ft x 1.6ft) grid. The grid was filled with paper, in the manner of a traditional Japanese wall, which could in turn be used as a projection screen. The main walls, five meters high (16.5ft), ran both along the edges of the stand (where they could be deployed to enclose the whole space, creating a private area) and within it, isolating or opening out specific locations within the stand.

The VIP lounge in its 'closed' state

client: **Mercedes-Benz**

fair: **Paris Motor Show**

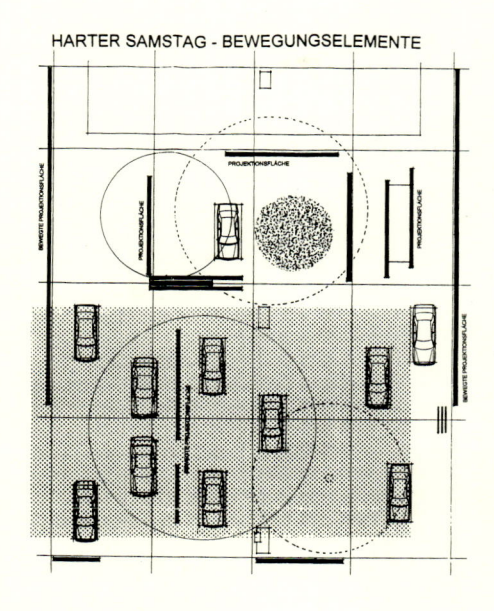

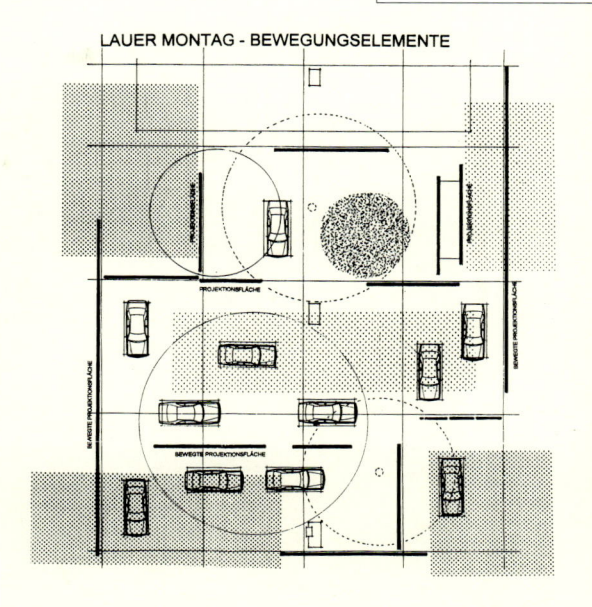

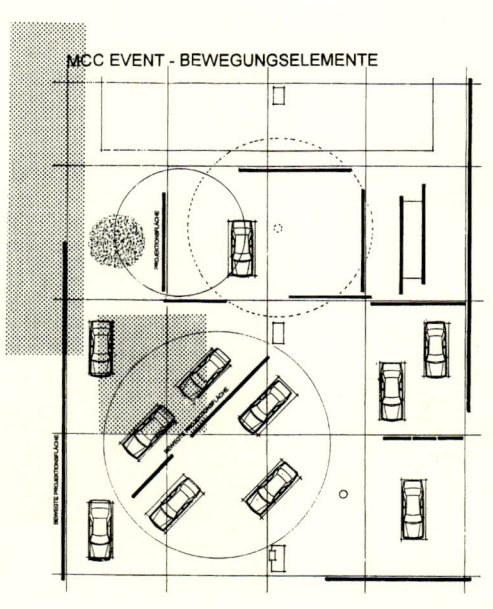

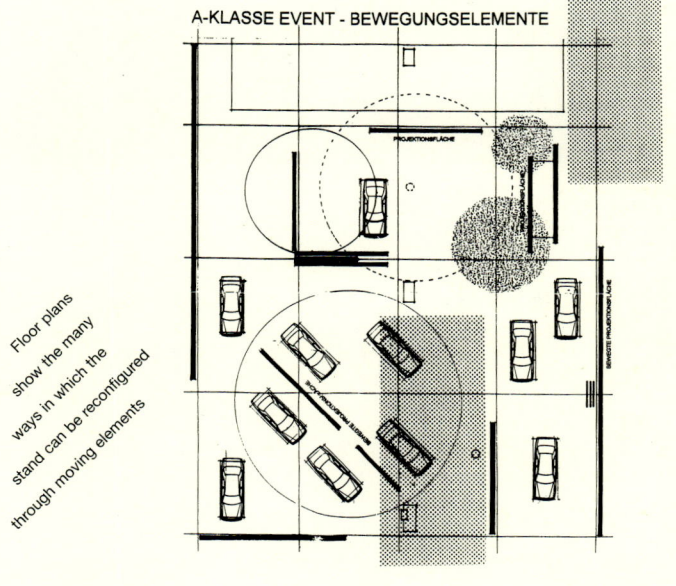

HARTER SAMSTAG - BEWEGUNGSELEMENTE

LAUER MONTAG - BEWEGUNGSELEMENTE

MCC EVENT - BEWEGUNGSELEMENTE

A-KLASSE EVENT - BEWEGUNGSELEMENTE

Floor plans show the many ways in which the stand can be reconfigured through moving elements

The umbrella ceiling when folded

A consequence of creating a dynamic space strongly identified by walls and floors was that the ceiling area which is normally abandoned to service needs, had to be involved in the concept. Here huge fabric umbrellas were installed, eight meters high (26ft), which unfurled and moved around the stand to highlight specific areas.

97

client: **Mercedes-Benz**

fair: **Paris Motor Show**

Mercedes-Benz Showroom

As part of the overall concept, a version of the stand was also built at Mercedes-Benz's Paris showroom on the Champs Élysées, and connected to the fair stand by a permanent video link – visitors to the showroom were taking part in the stand and vice versa.

The Paris Mercedes-Benz stand shows both extreme ingenuity in conception, and great technical skill in execution. It was an ambitious and highly successful project, widely admired by visitors to the event and by other professionals in the exhibition field.

The Champs Élysées showroom with video link to the fair

The Motor Sport exhibition in an adjoining hall used the same design theme

intel®

client: Intel, Santa Clara, California, USA

designer: Rouse-Wyatt Associates, Cincinnati, Ohio, USA
Denby Associates, Princeton, New Jersey, USA

product/service: Computer, networking and communication products

fair: USA Tour

date: 1996–1998 (ongoing)

On February 6th 1996 what has been called the world's largest traveling exhibition opened in Los Angeles, California – it celebrated the 150th anniversary of the foundation of the Smithsonian Institution. This exhibition is set to visit 11 other cities around the USA by the end of January 1998. The 'America's Smithsonian' traveling exhibit includes over 300 treasures, and features such items as paintings by Edward Hopper and Mary Cassatt, as well as historic documents, natural relics and technological inventions.

client: **Intel**

fair: **Ongoing USA Tour**

stand size: **15.25m x 18m (50ft x 60ft) enclosed stand**
total production time: **9 months**

INTEL

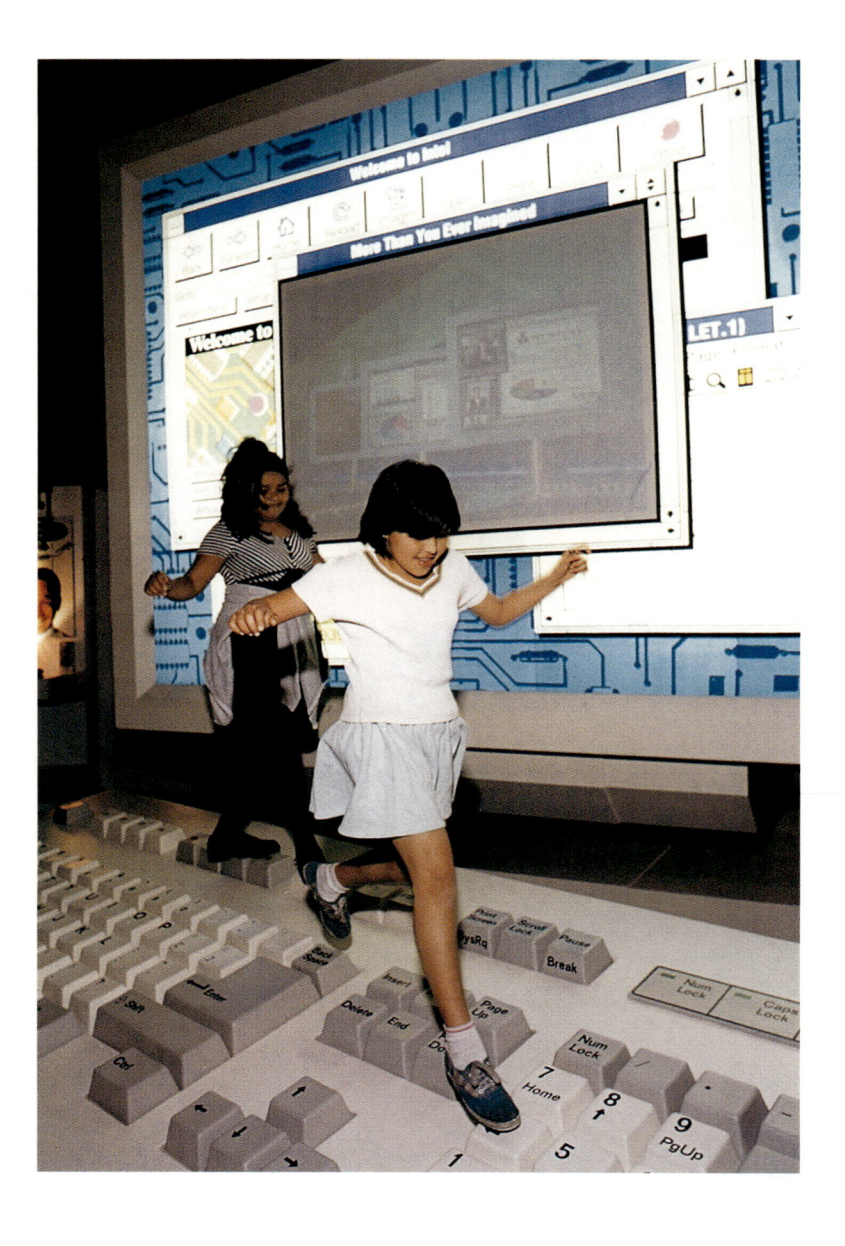

The computer-chip company Intel is one of the main sponsors of the exhibition. Its support is not only financial but practical: it provided computing equipment to help design the floor plan of the main exhibition, and to create the World Wide Web site that celebrates and commemorates the 'America's Smithsonian' exhibit. Intel is also sponsoring a children's competition called the 'Invention of the Future' contest (to encourage student's science and math skills) and organizing computer learning events for parents, teachers and students in schools near the exhibition venues. And Intel's support is highlighted by Intel's own exhibition which accompanies the main show.

client: **Intel**

fair: **Ongoing USA Tour**

A giant desktop, including the coffee mug, is the key exterior theme

Expressing sponsorship support for a major cultural event through a linked exhibit is the main aim.

The Intel exhibition aims to show visitors how the computer works and the role of the microprocessor in the modern computer: Intel manufactures computer chips as a major part of its business. 'Our exhibit allows visitors to **get to know computing** on a whole new level' states Dr Andrew S. Grove, Intel's president and CEO. 'The personal computer has come a long way since its roots as a calculating device. It is becoming the tool we use to communicate – using words, pictures and sounds – with our families, friends and colleagues around the world.'

101

client: **Intel**

fair: **Ongoing USA Tour**

This has been achieved by building a giant, walk-in model of a computer, with a 14-foot-high monitor, giant keyboard and motherboard. As visitors walk through, over and around these elements, interactive multimedia is used to communicate additional information, using the host character of 'Chip, the Microprocessor' and telling the story of the past, present and future of the Information Age.

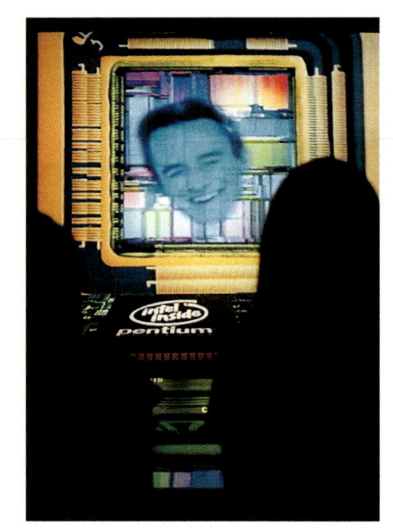

'Chip, the Microprocessor' leads the onscreen commentary

At the center of the exhibition is a walk-in hard drive featuring an environmental theater with a presentation entitled '**More Than You Ever Imagined**'. And at the close of the exhibition visitors get the opportunity to experiment hands-on with new computer technologies – using video phones, surfing the Internet and test-driving new software applications.

The key problem for a multi-site exhibition is logistics

client: **Intel**

fair: **Ongoing USA Tour**

client: **Intel**

fair: **Ongoing USA Tour**

The giant PC, demo stations and booth structure were designed by *Denby Associates* in New Jersey, USA. The theater presentation and stage were created for Intel by *Rouse-Wyatt Associates* in Ohio, USA. They used as a model Intel's television advertising for their Pentium and other microchip products, which features a 'flight' through the interior of a computer to home in on the microprocessor, carrying Intel's key slogan 'Intel Inside'. However, beyond this, the line devised by the designers and Intel is deliberately subtle. The Intel name is not mentioned during any of the audio presentations, nor is it shown on the theater screen.

The visit ends with a hands-on area to experience the Internet

client: **Intel**

fair: **Ongoing USA Tour**

Hands-on opportunities reinforce the message presented

An indirect approach to presenting the product strengthens its market inevitability.

The **indirect approach** used here has splendid antecedents in military history, from Clausewitz to Liddell Hart. Here it could be described as a politic of inevitability, Intel does not need to shout that its equipment is the best: it has, after all, been behind the main developments in microchips for the last decade. So its tactic is one of express understatement.

105

client: **Intel**

fair: **Ongoing USA Tour**

Inside the multimedia theater

This shows through even in positioning its celebration of the exhibition behind the main display, while supporting it with outreach activities such as 'PC Dads' and the 'Invention of the Future' contest for schoolchildren. In terms of assessing the success of the design, this apparently relaxed approach needs to be contrasted with the logistical complexities of designing a stand that can be dismounted and remounted 22 times in two years and be maintained efficiently during each city's approximate four-week run. The Intel fanfare for the Smithsonian event is a key example of mature marketing, and of developmental excellence in achievement.

client: Ericsson Mobile Communications AB, Stockholm, Sweden
designer: Imagination, London, UK
product/service: Telecommunications
fair: CeBIT Hanover, Germany
date: 1996 and 1997

Ericsson do not only sell mobile phones; rather they see themselves as being in the business of voice transmission. The distinction is a subtle one. It is more than the difference between selling a product and offering a service. It is a statement about what is increasingly termed 'the brand experience' – the total package of product, service, image and care, delivered to the client by the company, not only through a commercial relationship, but also by the advertising and corporate image of the company.

client: **Ericsson Mobile Communications**

fair: **CeBIT Hanover**

stand size: **Two-tier island stand**

total production time: **5 months**

ERICSSON

Ericsson turned to the London design group *Imagination* for help with their stand at CeBIT, the major European IT, computer and telecommunications trade show. They were launching the new 300 series family of mobile phone products, as well as the 'Life' concept. *Imagination* took the view that 'life meant live' and planned a stand that included a series of eight-minute **performances** by acrobats on a frame over the launch area for the three new products. Alongside the performances was a continuous video show of three lifestyle films, created by *Imagination*, showing the Ericsson mobile phone range in use in everyday situations. The acrobats' **control, flexibility and communication** were the same qualities that the Ericsson products embodied.

General view of the stand at CeBIT '96

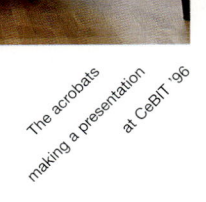

client: **Ericsson Mobile Communications**

fair: **CeBIT Hanover**

'Life means live.'

The acrobats making a presentation at CeBIT '96

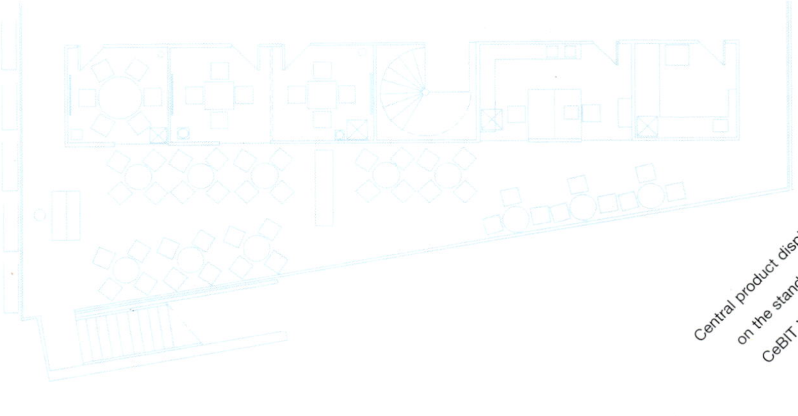

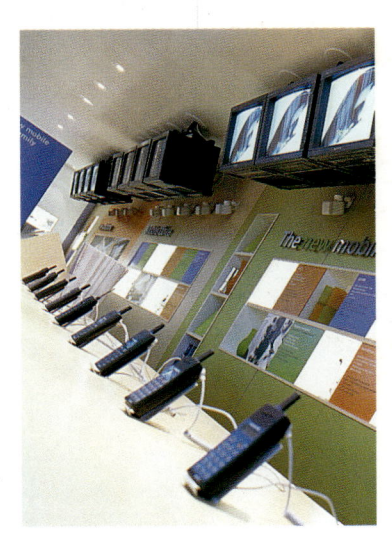

Central product display on the stand at CeBIT '96

109

client: **Ericsson Mobile Communications**

fair: **CeBIT Hanover**

The thinking behind the design approach was the intention of shifting client perceptions from that of a corporate multinational communications supplier to a customer-oriented mobile communications brand name. The stand represented the culmination of a complete campaign using a combination of integrated media strategies, starting with pre-launch poster and press advertising, through to the production of a feature show, a series of films, multimedia design, graphics and literature for the event itself. This planning and management succ- eeded in bringing the brand to life over a six-day period. It created the upbeat feeling necessary to demonstrate Ericsson's under- standing and appreciation of mod- ern lifestyles within a contemporary environment.

Supporting graphics at CeBIT '96

Graphic display at CeBIT '96: note the use of wall-washing light

The press pack

The 'Life' brochure for CeBIT '96

client: **Ericsson Mobile Communications**

fair: **CeBIT Hanover**

Outside sites used for poster displays to support the 'Life' theme during CeBIT '96

Innovative creative solutions to bring a brand to life.

Documentation wall at CeBIT '96

'Life' also meant taking the message beyond the stand. *Imagination* commissioned a series of posters which were shown on over 250 **outdoor** sites in Hanover before and during the CeBIT show, not only encouraging visitors to come to the stand, but also expressing the **everyday validity** of the Ericsson proposal. Other graphic support came from local press advertising, and an Ericsson 'Life' brochure, distributed at the show. Music CDs and photo CD-ROMs were produced for handing out on the stand, together with postcards and carrier bags. These postcards were also handed out around Hanover's mainline rail station, where a 2.5-meter high (8ft) ice sculpture of the new Ericsson GH388 phone was displayed (CeBIT takes place in winter!).

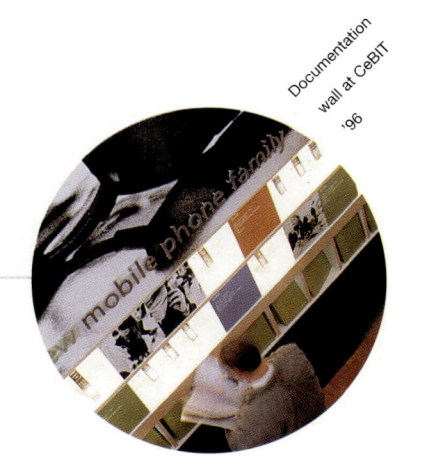

client: **Ericsson Mobile Communications**

fair: **CeBIT Hanover**

Performance artists turn a static structure into a dramatic moving poster at CeBIT '96

112

client: **Ericsson Mobile Communications**

fair: **CeBIT Hanover**

The Ericsson stand shows how stand design alone is not enough to convey a complex message, but needs to be supported by a wide-ranging strategy. The integration of these elements is what spells success. Polls taken at the fair suggested that over 50 per cent of visitors had the highest awareness of the stand, and a similar proportion had visited the stand.

The acrobats are back – this time with jazz in support at CeBIT '96

113

client: **Ericsson Mobile Communications**

fair: **CeBIT Hanover**

The 'Voice' theme presented Ericsson at CeBIT '97

The CeBIT stand happened at a time when Ericsson was reviewing its global brand and communications strategy in order to adapt to a more customer-focused market. The stand provided a catalyst in this process, creating a ripple of confidence through the whole company. Thus a **double objective** was achieved: of increasing awareness of the brand both within the professional market represented by the event, and within the company globally. *Imagination*'s creative solutions have led not only to a commission to create the mobile communications stand for CeBIT '97, where 'Voice' was used as the main theme, but also for the principal corporate stand at that event. *Imagination* have also been retained as leading consultants to the company for their overall exhibition strategy.

114

client: Virgin Interactive Entertainment, London, UK
designer: Root Associates, London, UK
product/service: Computer games
fair: Electronic Computer Trade Show, Olympia, London
date: September 1996

The ECTS show is the most important professional event for the computer entertainment industry in Europe, covering computer games, music and interactive media. It creates an opportunity for producers, buyers, suppliers and the press to meet and look at new trends and products. Most companies exhibiting have a series of meetings with clients and customers planned well in advance, as well as showcasing new products to potential new clients. Virgin Interactive Entertainment, now part of the VIACOM group, create computer games, including the very successful Command and Conquer series.

client: **Virgin Interactive Entertainment**

fair: **Electronic Computer Trade Show**

stand size: **Enclosed stand: 300 square meters (985 square feet) on two tiers**

total production time: **3 months**

VIRGIN INTERACTIVE ENTERTAINMENT

The functional aspect of the brief to *Root Associates* was therefore to provide both a showroom area and a suite of private meeting rooms. The site size was 300 square meters (985 square feet), and the construction could be on two levels. The visual aspect of the brief was summed up by VIE's (Virgin Interactive Entertainment) marketing department as **'The Virgin Brotherhood'** with a Gothic theme as a key. *Root Associates* delivered a dominating mock-medieval castle, with gaping gargoyles, ogival arches and attendant's in hooded monkish robes.

'The Virgin Brotherhood – Join us.'

General view of the stand from above

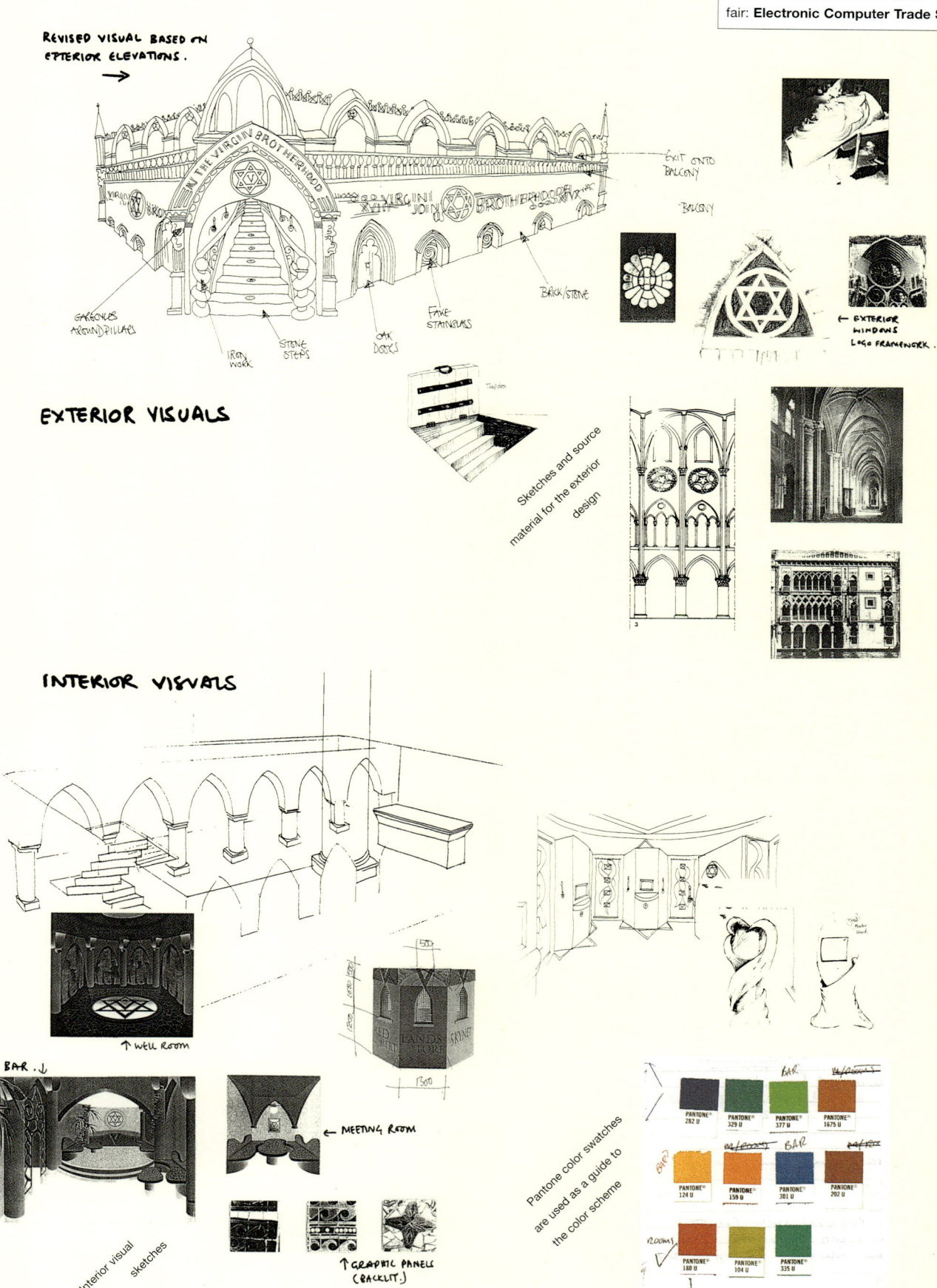

client: **Virgin Interactive Entertainment**

fair: **Electronic Computer Trade Show**

REVISED VISUAL BASED ON EXTERIOR ELEVATIONS.

EXIT ONTO BALCONY

BALCONY

← EXTERIOR WINDOWS LOGO FRAMEWORK.

GARGOYLES AROUND PILLARS

IRON WORK

STONE STEPS

OAK DOORS

FAKE STAINGLASS

BRICK/STONE

EXTERIOR VISUALS

Sketches and source material for the exterior design

INTERIOR VISUALS

↑ WELL ROOM

BAR ↓

← MEETING ROOM

↑ GRAPHIC PANELS (BACKLIT)

Interior visual sketches

Pantone color swatches are used as a guide to the color scheme

BAR			
PANTONE 282 U	PANTONE 329 U	PANTONE 377 U	PANTONE 1675 U

BAR	BAR		
PANTONE 124 U	PANTONE 158 U	PANTONE 301 U	PANTONE 202 U

ROOMS			
PANTONE 188 U	PANTONE 104 U	PANTONE 335 U	

117

client: **Virgin Interactive Entertainment**

fair: **Electronic Computer Trade Show**

In terms of space planning, *Root Associates*, in association with builders Pico Ltd., decided that a closed stand would be best, with a single main entrance leading to a showcase area on the upper floor, and then down into the meeting room area on the ground floor. The design thus controlled the visitors' main itinerary through the stand.

As to the look of the stand, the designer's first task was to create the 'Brotherhood Manifesto'. This document, by setting out the **objectives of the approach**, defined the parameters for the design, and also provided a series of texts that were incorporated into the final design, screen-printed onto linen banners, and hung in the main display area. Work also went ahead on a logotype and a series of branding proposals.

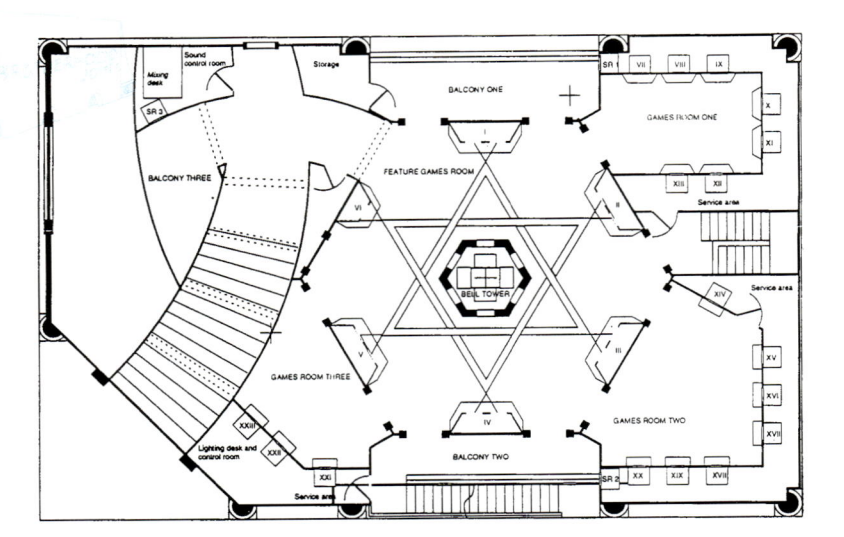

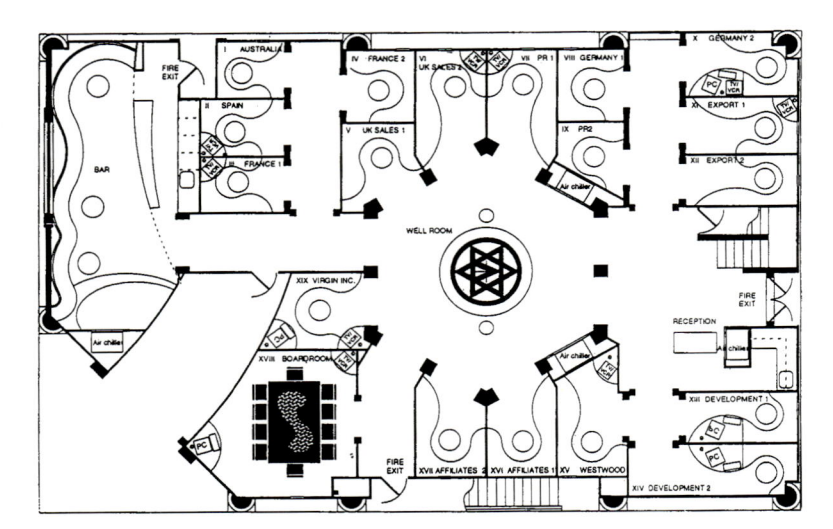

The Virgin Interactive stand plan for the upper level (top) and the lower level (bottom)

'The Virgin Brotherhood Manifesto' banner

client: **Virgin Interactive Entertainment**

fair: **Electronic Computer Trade Show**

The visual designs for the logo were developed through studying historical examples of star-shaped badges, incorporating a version of Virgin's capital 'V' trademark, and finding appropriate lettering to give a stone-carved look. The final logo was embossed in a stone or metal finish, as appropriate.

Creating 'The Virgin Brotherhood' brand

The creation of atmosphere – down to controlled air-conditioning – was a key premise in the effect of the stand.

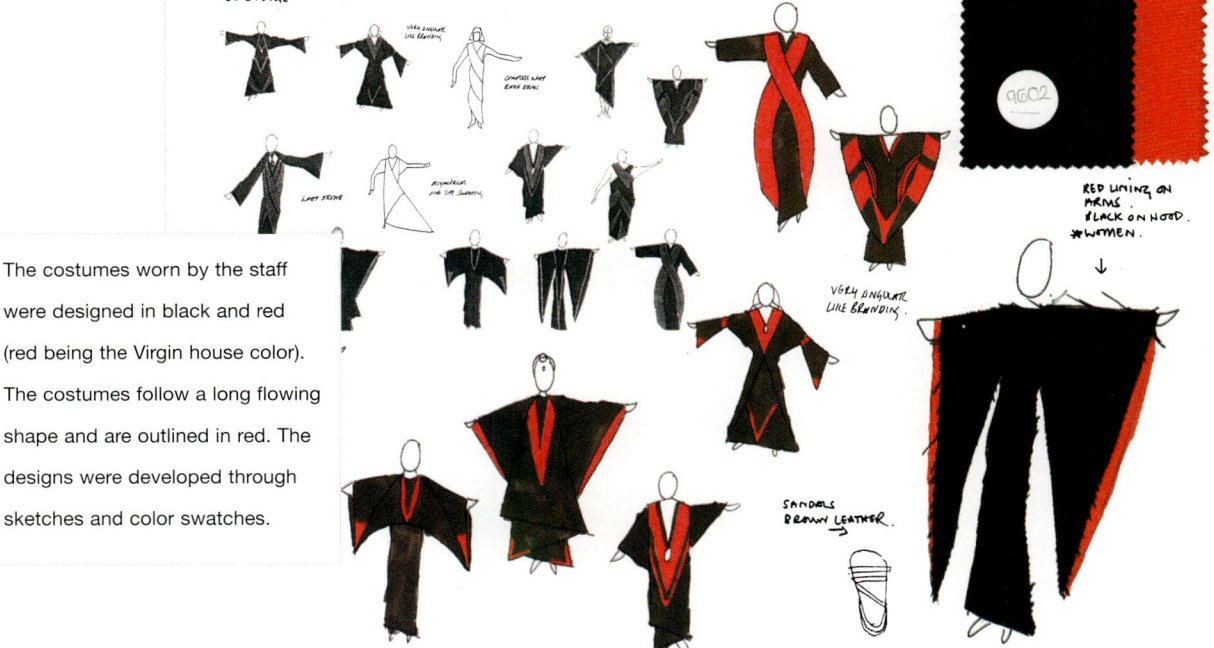

The costumes worn by the staff were designed in black and red (red being the Virgin house color). The costumes follow a long flowing shape and are outlined in red. The designs were developed through sketches and color swatches.

119

client: **Virgin Interactive Entertainment**

fair: **Electronic Computer Trade Show**

The stand has an open entrance area on one corner, where a flight of dark gray stairs leads up to the first floor display area. Here three games rooms were set out to display the current product range, with a feature game area immediately by the stairhead to show the latest product, Red Alert (which went on to sell over 500,000 copies in its first week of release). In each games area a series of wall-mounted consoles allowed visitors waiting for appointments to try out the products. Between the games areas large screen projectors showed a continuous video, commissioned by the designers, on the new theme. The central feature of the first floor was the bell tower. At the opposite side of the stand from the stairhead was the stairway down to the meeting area. While very **richly colored throughout** – as compared to the tones of gray and white used on the exterior – the upper floor was less strongly colored than the lower area.

The main entrance

The first floor area

Detail over the main entrance

client: **Virgin Interactive Entertainment**

fair: **Electronic Computer Trade Show**

Attention to detail – the costumes, the hinges on the press pack, the live snake – made the stand convincing and memorable.

The ground floor was a dark crypt-like space, heavily tinted in red and gold. In the center was the well with a lid in the star pattern used on the logo. The water in the well bubbled and turned red, while a bell tolled the hours. To reinforce the Gothic theme, air coolers were installed in the ground floor area to maintain a temperature level several degrees below that of the showcase area.

The main area on the lower level

The well in the lower area

Around the well were 18 individual meeting areas, a boardroom (complete with glass-topped table incorporating a moving, live snake) and a bar area. Background walls in the meeting areas carried graphic panels illuminated from behind. Technical and lighting control for the whole space was run from a control room on the upper floor.

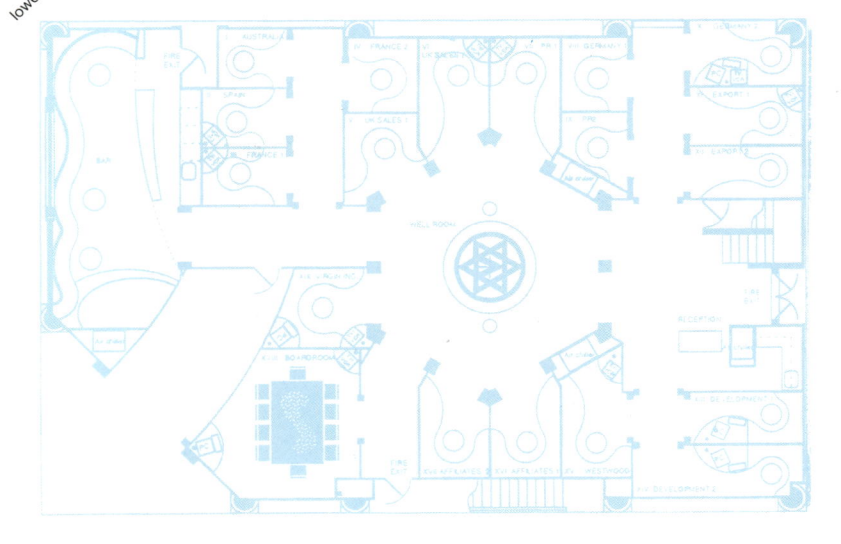

client: **Virgin Interactive Entertainment**

fair: **Electronic Computer Trade Show**

The design of the exterior was deliberately monochromatic, so increasing the contrast with the richly-colored interior. Design elements for the Gothic façades were developed from photographs and sketches of medieval originals, but the central visual feature was the pair of immense gargoyles flanking the entrance. The walls were in plaster rendered to look like stone blocks, with statements from the manifesto lettered onto darker mock-stone panels. Details such as air-conditioning outlets (a rare feature in 14th century monasteries) were framed in darker brick.

Air-conditioning, medieval style

Exterior details

The corner gargoyle

client: **Virgin Interactive Entertainment**

fair: **Electronic Computer Trade Show**

Once the creative work had been done and worked through in a series of meetings with the clients, the whole design had to be drawn up to scale for fabrication. Following this, lighting, electrical circuits and systems facilities were planned. The designers also worked with the construction team, headed by Pico Ltd., on the assembly and disassembly requirements, and commissioned the molding of gargoyles, the making up of costumes, and the printing of banners. The designers were also responsible for designing and planning the staff T-shirts and business cards, incorporating the new logo, and the press pack, presented as a handcrafted package in a linen bag.

Press pack with product list

'Trade fair design is not a stand-alone business.'

Virgin Interactive considered the stand a great success. It was visually different from the surrounding stands, and functioned, despite its complexity, extremely well for the endless series of meetings held with hundreds of clients and visitors through the fair. *Root Associates* not only came up with a wholly original visual solution, but carried this through to a fine level of detail. Martin Root, founder of the company, points out that 'trade fair design is not a stand-alone business. It demands a wide range of skills, and focused teamwork. Above all, to be successful requires a clear understanding of the client's needs and ideas, and good cooperation with them.' *Root Associates*' reputation for their stand design work is only part of a larger portfolio of successful client relationships and projects.

123

4 Beyond the Stand

The concept of the exhibition stand as a display of products and services for clients, customers or the public, does not have to be tied to an annual week in Las Vegas, Frankfurt, Tokyo or Milan. These three projects show the idea of the stand being turned into either a permanent or a moveable site, and look at some of the problems and opportunities this poses.

For Pilkington, a leading glass manufacturer, the problem was in part one of the size and complexity of their products. They decided to create a permanent site at their factory where they could demonstrate the range and quality of their specialized products to selected clients in their own time. Just as an appointments system at a trade fair creates a fixed time for a meeting, so a permanent site creates both a special atmosphere and quality time for a meeting.

For *RedFish Communications*, the model was the public exhibition event. Their brief was to publicize the release on video of George Lucas' Star Wars trilogy, and then in 1997 the re-release of the film in cinemas. For this they decided to build a mobile unit, which was used to travel the country using outdoor sites to spread the word about the 'Force'.

Gardner Merchant already had a training facility for the restaurants they supply and service for companies, hospitals and schools. They decided to upgrade this into a permanent marketing center, where there is both an exhibition area setting out the services that they offer, and a suite of scaled down restaurants where clients can enjoy the Gardner Merchant experience in real life.

These projects show how design transfer skills operate, taking the ability to work in one context into another. This is achieved by seeing the brief from the client as being open-ended, and capable of different solutions and interpretations.

PILKINGTON

client: Pilkington plc, Lathom, UK
designer: Communication by Design, London, UK
product/service: Glass manufacturer
fair: Pilkington Technology Centre, Lathom UK
date: 1995

Pilkington is one of the world leaders in glass technology, and has a strong record in product innovation. To present their widely different range of products to target key partners and clients, they decided that a permanent gallery at their Lancashire factory was the best solution. A permanent exhibit has the advantage over a temporary exhibition site. However, at the same time, the site has to be treated as a long-term event, with the capacity to evolve and change with new developments in the corporate client's business.

client: **Pilkington plc**
fair: **Pilkington Technology Centre**
stand size: **Permanent structure on two levels**
total production time: **Continuously evolving**

PILKINGTON

Geoff Aldridge, of *Communication by Design*, was invited by Pilkington to take up the challenge of modernizing and refitting an existing on-site display in 1994. The existing arrangement of space consisted of a ground floor reception and foyer area, linked by a staircase and a short corridor to a large room with a closed auditorium at its center. The system was designed for **guided visits** with a presenter, who would explain the individual displays – this approach was retained in the refitting of the display. This in turn meant that the exhibition space was divided into three key areas: the foyer space (where visitors would wait before a visit), the corridor space, and the space around the auditorium on the upper floor. Each of these needed individual treatment.

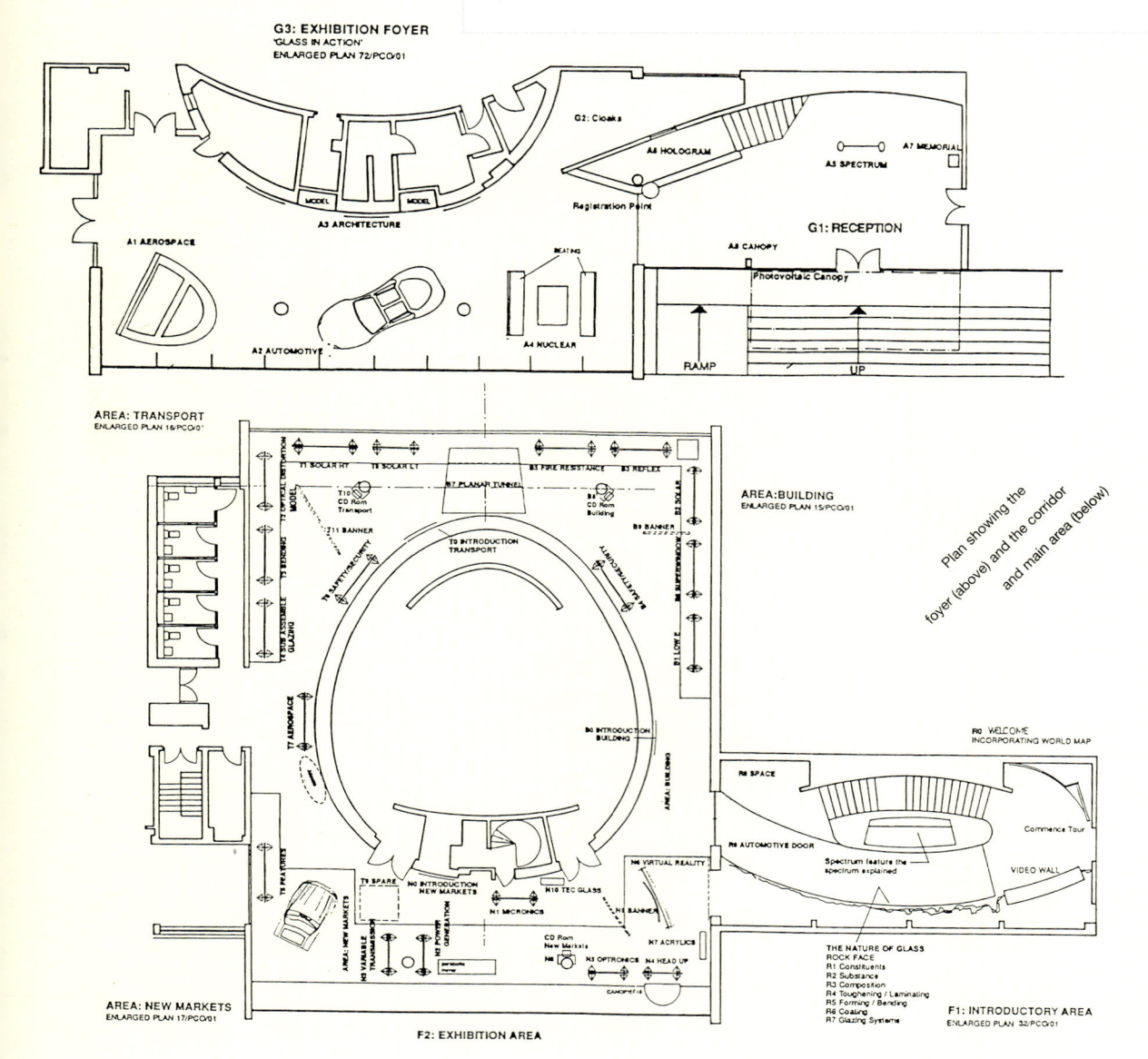

Plan showing the foyer (above) and the corridor and main area (below)

client: **Pilkington plc**

fair: **Pilkington Technology Centre**

Technology is at the heart of the client's business.

The site for the exhibit was set among the general factory buildings: it was also the main visitor reception for the site. One of the first decisions made was that it should be visually strengthened from the exterior, so providing a focus. The reception area was in fact in a link building joining two larger structures. While a major structural alteration was not possible, the exhibition block itself and the reception area were given new façades to unify them, and distinguish them from the surrounding buildings. Part of the car park was grassed over, and a flag-pole erected, to create a more formal and welcoming setting. Over the reception area entrance, a photo-voltaic glass canopy was mounted, which would automatically lighten or darken according to the level of sunlight.

The exterior of the center before and after the redesign

Glass as a communication medium or a structural element.

Within the entrance, foyer and exhibition space, particular attention was paid to wall surfaces, and glass was introduced as a communication or structural medium wherever possible. For example, a large glass sheet etched with a map of the world hangs above the reception desk, indicating Pilkington's manufacturing and sales locations worldwide, and the treads on the staircase leading to the corridor are made from bare, toughened glass.

client: **Pilkington plc**

fair: **Pilkington Technology Centre**

The foyer area from outside, at night

Geoff Aldridge – as part of a study group from the design agency and the clients – decided that the foyer area would best be given over to three static physical exhibits showing the **range of applications** of Pilkington's products, together with an interactive display of other applications through a computer screen. Since the area had an external glass wall and an internal curved wall, the latter was the obvious site for the computer screen, with adjoining space for models or graphic displays. The three key products featured were protective glass for the nuclear industry, automotive glass, with a full-size rally car, and glass used in aerospace technology, with a fighter cockpit.

Three static physical exhibits showing the range of applications.

client: **Pilkington plc**

fair: **Pilkington Technology Centre**

The corridor space was used to present the history and basic concepts of the glass industry, through a wall of stone into which were embedded, or on which were displayed, examples of early Egyptian glass, and the chemical compounds that make up glass, together with a series of video screens showing short explanatory videos. This area was deliberately darkened, so that lighting effects could be used to present each phase. At the end of the corridor a pair of glazed automatic doors led into the main exhibition space. For these doors U-Mu glass was used – it has the special property of remaining opaque until charged electrically, when it becomes transparent. So the presenter would, at the flick of a switch, literally enlighten the visitors as to what lay beyond, an effective *coup de théâtre*.

On the rock-face – the corridor leading to the main display area

client: **Pilkington plc**

fair: **Pilkington Technology Centre**

If the foyer display was self-communicating, and the corridor was a fixed, presented, historical display, then the main exhibition area in contrast needed the potential of flexibility. *Communication by Design* created a system of chromed steel and glass tables for each exhibit, so that items could be added or changed without interrupting the visual flow of the whole presentation. These displays featured the strength of safety glass (with a mannequin carrying weights standing on a sheet of glass), thermally insulated super-windows (using a triple layer of glass for insulation), a planar tunnel of darkened mirror glass in which the viewer's reflection would be invisible, and displays of optically corrected curved glass, such as those used in the motor industry.

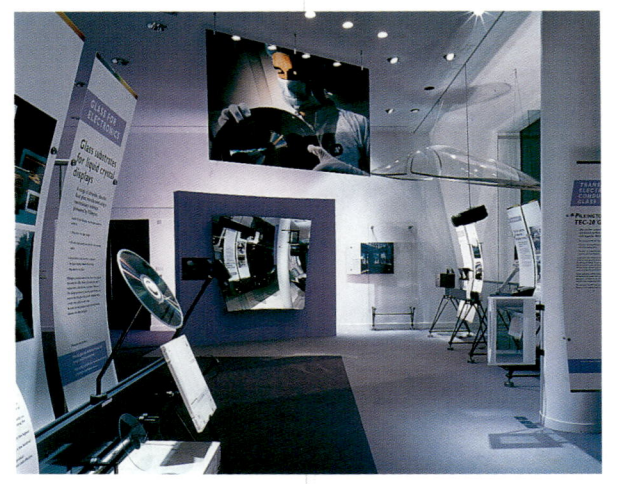

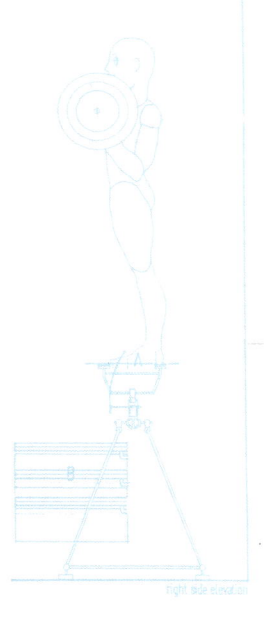

General views of the display area

A permanent event of this kind sits between traditional fair stand design and full-blown interior architecture. In conceiving it, Geoff Aldridge and his colleagues balanced the positive aspects of permanence – installing elements such as the photovoltaic canopy – and allowing for the site to develop over time, by creating a flexible display system in the main area.

The center opened in late 1995, and has already welcomed a large number of visitors, from delegations of overseas clients, to Members of Parliament to professional researchers. It was short-listed for a 1996 Design Effectiveness Award, and Geoff Aldridge now sits on a committee formed by Pilkington to oversee and guide the future development of the Technology Centre.

client: Fox Video, London, UK

designer: RedFish Communications Ltd., London, UK

photographer: Steve Day for RedFish Communications Ltd.

product/service: Star Wars Video Promotion vehicle

fair: Touring around the UK

date: 1995

Star Wars returns! Lucasfilm decided to re-release the videos of the first three Star Wars films in autumn 1995, while at the same time confirming that a further new title was already in production. In 1997, re-edited and extended versions of the first three titles were also released. *RedFish Communications* were asked in 1995 by the UK distributors, Fox Video, to organize a nationwide promotion for these video releases. With only a couple of weeks notice, Darth Vader was to strut his stuff once more!

client: **Fox Video**

fair: **Touring around the UK**

stand size: **Self-contained unit on 13.5m (44ft) trailer**

total production time: **Under ten days**

FOX VIDEO

While actors and props were available, and a short scenario using dialog from the film quickly written, hiring halls or spaces for events around the country simply could not be done within the **time-scale**. Instead, Kevin Stokes of *RedFish* contacted Torton Bodies, **specialist** builders of display and promotional vehicles. He arranged for them to take delivery of a full-scale mock-up of an X-WING fighter, which Torton mounted into an open-sided 13.5m (44ft) trailer. Ramps were built to allow Vader and his escort of Imperial Guards to move on and off the 'set', and large-screen television monitors were built into the side of the vehicle to project images from the films and advertising for the video releases.

'Celebrating the re-launch of the Star Wars Trilogy.'

The 1995 exterior trailer livery

client: **Fox Video**

fair: **Touring around the UK**

Lord Vader takes the stage

client: **Fox Video**

fair: **Touring around the UK**

The vehicle under construction

Schematic drawing showing the fighter open on the trailer

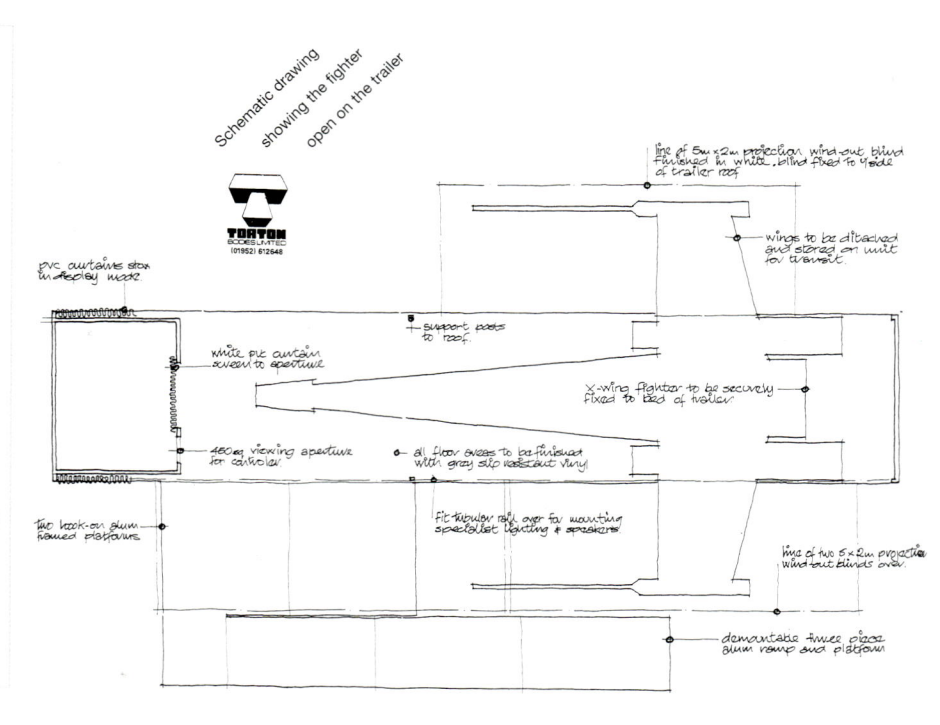

The whole design and building process took under ten days. As Clive Andrews from Torton Bodies explained: 'there was no time to prepare and submit design drawings. Our designers did a rough sketch, which our technical team checked for building effectiveness. This mainly concerned getting the X-WING onto an appropriate position on the trailer, positioning the television screens and arranging the ramps and lighting. Then the client came up on-site, and we built the whole thing by rule of thumb.'

client: **Fox Video**

fair: **Touring around the UK**

The vehicle made a two-month tour of Britain in 1995, stopping at festivals and in pre-determined supermarket car parks, and presenting four 20-minute 'performances'. Assembling and de-rigging the set took a few hours, so several sites could be covered in a day.

'The Imperial Invasion is coming to your galaxy.' 1995 strapline.

Vader and Imperial Guards – note the use of theatrical colored lighting

Darth meets the people

client: **Fox Video**

fair: **Touring around the UK**

Competition winners get a seat in the X-WING

The new exterior livery

For the 1997 release of the new version of *Star Wars*, RedFish arranged for the vehicle to be upgraded and then set out a further two-month tour. New video consoles for games related to the Star Wars trilogy were installed at the rear of the vehicle, and access to the pilot's seat of the X-WING fighter was improved, and the external livery was repainted. The success of this further tour was highlighted both by a television appearance for the vehicle, and in more concrete terms by very positive results for Toys 'R' Us, who had co-sponsored the tour, commissioned by Fox Film Company.

As an example of a **professional technical team** working fast on a single creative idea, the Star Wars vehicle is excellent. Mobile displays, whether opening as a proscenium, as in this case, or in the form of meeting rooms within closed but expandable vehicles, offer a way of bringing a product or service to the attention of a large number of people in different locations very quickly. They can be seen as a trade fair stand on wheels.

GARDNER MERCHANT

client: Gardner Merchant plc, London, UK

designer: Marketplace Design, Abingdon, UK

product/service: UK's largest contract caterer

fair: Permanent food court and gallery

date: Ongoing

Gardner Merchant are in the food business. Among other activities, Gardner Merchant's main role is in supplying catering facilities to other companies' factories and offices, as well as to the educational and health-care sector. The days of the works canteen, with gray Formica tables, strip lighting, serving hatches and the 'chow line' are long gone: companies now want a wider choice, not only in catering, but in the atmosphere and ambience of their eateries. But how to show prospective clients the range of services that Gardner Merchant could offer, other than through a slide show or a series of visits to existing sites?

client: **Gardner Merchant plc**
fair: **Permanent food court and gallery**

stand size: **361 square meters (1,185 square feet) permanent exhibition area**

total production time: **9 months**

GARDNER MERCHANT

Framing the 'branded offer' in a permanent setting.

Gardner Merchant have a variety of 'branded offers' – ranging from a coffee bar, Café Toscana, to Oriental Express, Pizza Gusta, and Explorers – offering food from around the world. The package includes not only the interior decoration of the site, but complete kitchen equipment, training and management, food delivery services and packaging, right down to staff uniforms. The company already had a training facility at Kenley, and decided to upgrade this. They commissioned *Marketplace Design* in Abingdon to work with them on the project.

General view of the completed gallery

client: **Gardner Merchant plc**

fair: **Permanent food court and gallery**

Presentation drawings showing the different activity areas of the gallery

The proposal that emerged was for a two-zone presentation area – the gallery and the food court. The gallery would be a walk-through exhibition area, which would present the range of services the client had on offer via graphics and interactive screens. In the food court, visitors would see a series of **fully-operational** but scaled-down examples of Gardner Merchant's restaurant brands (and food facilities, such as the Strollers Deli), as well as a new training kitchen.

client: **Gardner Merchant plc**

fair: **Permanent food court and gallery**

Presentation area in the gallery showing the special furniture

In the gallery, which was framed by the historic interior of Kenley House, the designers created a series of furniture units, such as reception desks and seating, together with display modules. (The display modules ranged from panels for graphics and monitor towers, to supports for the video presentations.) The exhibition is designed as a **walk-through**, either independently or with a guide. It is adjacent to the food court.

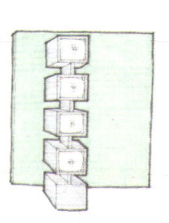

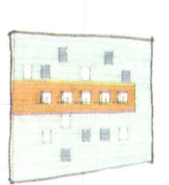

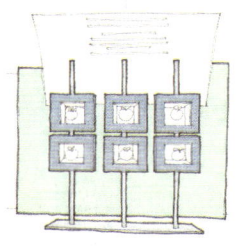

Detailed studies for permanent display constructions in the gallery

140

client: **Gardner Merchant plc**

fair: **Permanent food court and gallery**

The food court is a set of small restaurant suites and a retail shop, which shows the many branded food offers available from Gardner Merchant. These are delivered to the client as **complete packages**, including complete design and installation, menus, food deliveries and training. The food court comprises several small restaurant units, showing the liveries, seating and serving arrangements, and a typical range of the food on offer.

'What you see is what you get.'

The food court showing the branded food offers available

client: **Gardner Merchant plc**

fair: **Permanent food court and gallery**

During most of the week the food court is used as a training center for managers, chefs and support staff. And so, when clients come to see the exhibition area, they can be offered a meal in the restaurant that mainly interests them. The result is that Gardner Merchant not only have a completely updated **training** facility, but also a **marketing** unit which shows prospective clients 'what you see is what you get' in full scale.

Design and finished result in the gallery area

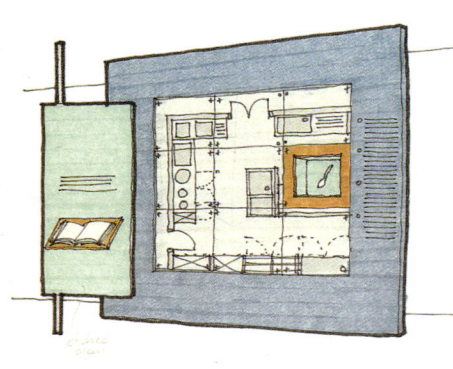

The gallery area is especially innovative, using **unique furniture designs** to create a mood that is expressly the client's own but melds with the traditional decoration of the formal house in which it is set. As a design solution it has the merit of taking the brief that necessary one step further.

Conclusion

What are the key qualities an expo designer should seek to develop?

The first, is technical skill: the ability to draw and visualize, and further than that to conceptualize three-dimensional spaces, and convey these to colleagues and clients through sketches and roughs. As you will have seen, many of the most successful projects in this book were created in very short time-scales. So being able to communicate quickly and graphically is very important.

The second, is imagination: the mental agility to dream up ideas and concepts. Even if these are not the right answers first time, the process of creating ideas drives the progress of the concept forward. Look at the way roughs and sketches have been used to develop concepts in these case-studies, and think about the kind of imaginative leaps involved in creating projects like 'Product Heaven' or the 'Woody' mobile.

The third, is communication: the ability to read a brief, comment on it, and read beyond it to the client's needs and ambitions, and communicate effectively with the client to achieve these. It is not surprising that some of the most ambitious projects here – work by *Imagination*, *Kauffmann Theilig & Partner*, or *Root Associates*, for example – comes from design agencies who have a broad base of skills, and are not just focused on events. This skill base enables them to deliver a larger package – with full video and graphics support, for example – and also brings a wider view of design potential to the help of the client.

The final, and most important quality, is organizational skill. Some of the projects we have seen here were executed to intensely tight deadlines, and in any event, the start-up time for trade shows is being reduced by the growing pressure on organizers to house more events. Solid technical knowledge, visual and communication skills need to be backed up by the ability to plan and execute complex schemes to a tight schedule.

As a final case-study, we look at the way a design group, whose maxim is to deliver the client message literally face to face, worked on a range of presentations from a sales conference to a public open-air event to reinforce a marketing message based on a very successful series of television commercials. *In Real Life*'s unorthodox approach created not only market success, but spread a new enthusiasm for the product through the company and to a broad general public. This total design approach shows how expo presentation skills can be adapted and extended to reach the widest of audiences, through originality, innovation and consummate execution.

At the heart of the expo or trade show is the visitor experience; what did the visitor gain? Was it a pleasant meeting with established clients, an opportunity to make new contacts, or a chance to meet old friends? Alternatively, did it provide the opportunity to explore a new area of products or services? The expo designer has to cater for all these, and for the wider interests of the client: it is an endless challenge. As one designer said to me, 'expo design is like living on a roller-coaster – always up, down and around. Dizzying! But I wouldn't get off it for the world.'

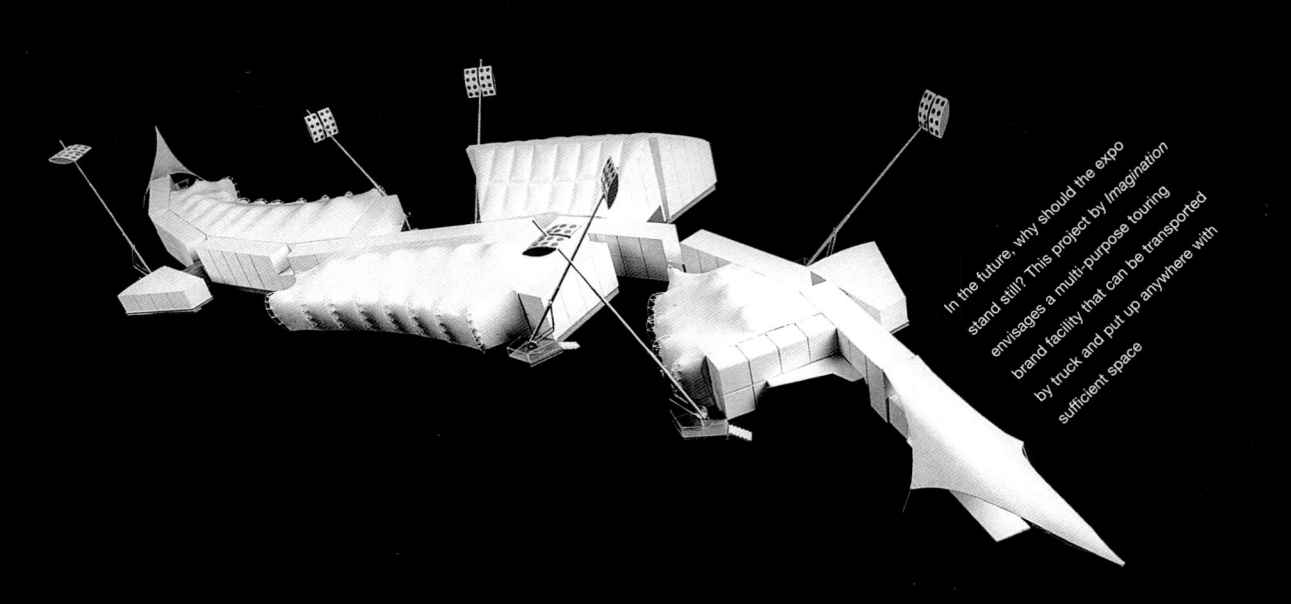

In the future, why should the expo stand still? This project by *Imagination* envisages a multi-purpose touring brand facility that can be transported by truck and put up anywhere with sufficient space

Tango

client: Britvic Soft Drinks Ltd., London, UK

designer: In Real Life, London, UK

product/service: Tango soft drinks

fair: Apple Tango Tongue outdoor promotion and related projects

date: 1996–1997

Britvic Soft Drinks Ltd. manufacture a range of soft drinks, mainly for the UK market. Their main brand, Orange Tango, had been repositioned within the market through a series of novel television commercials, and new packaging. What was needed now was to bring the other three flavors for Tango up to the same level of success as Orange Tango had reached.

client: **Britvic Soft Drinks Ltd.**
product: **Tango soft drinks**

TANGO

The advertising strategy, devised by *In Real Life*'s parent, the agency HHCL & Partners, led to the creation of a series of madcap and anarchic television commercials using the theme **'You know when you've been Tangoed!'**. The challenge to the creative team at *In Real Life* was to bring this to life in three-dimensional form within the company itself, towards its immediate trade market, and to the consuming public. This was achieved through a new approach to the sales conference, through a vehicle to bring the new product to the buyers, and through an astonishing public event, the Tango Tongue. The three events show how a fresh approach to design can help build a brand across a wide market, using an approach that puts the face-to-face trade fair experience at its center.

'You know when you've been Tangoed!'

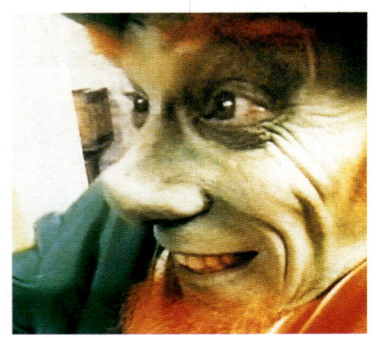

Television commercials put Tango over as a surprising and exciting product

146

client: **Britvic Soft Drinks Ltd.**

product: **Tango soft drinks**

The interior of the Tango Tongue mixes seduction and sensation through music, lights and a pulsating interior

client: **Britvic Soft Drinks Ltd.**
product: **Tango soft drinks**

fair: **Annual Sales Conference, ICC Birmingham, UK**
duration: **1 Day**
stand type: **Presentation stage**
stand size: **5m x 2.50m (16.5ft x 8.2ft)**
materials: **Stage, video wall, actors**
total production time: **6 weeks**

Tango Sales Conference

The sales conference was presented on a set in which presentation and live action were both of importance

'The process of transformation needed a theatrical solution to be effective.'

The conference theme was known by the umbrella term 'Operation Breakthrough', and included the new strategies for Tango, Pepsi and Robinsons. *In Real Life*'s initial brief from Britvic Soft Drinks Ltd. was to devise the annual sales conference that was to present the new concept. It is well known that the atmosphere of a sales conference can have a dramatic effect on performance in the following months: like the coach's pep talk before the team go out onto the field, it can spell victory if well done, or ensure defeat if inadequate.

| client: | **Britvic Soft Drinks Ltd.** |
| product: | **Tango soft drinks** |

In Real Life took the theme of **breakthrough** as the central concept by staging the conference as 'mission control', with participants debating and enacting ideas rather than just presenting. Innovative audiovisual and lighting techniques were used to create a flexible, dramatic context for this. This face-to-face approach involved all present actively in the process, as well as creating an individual visual environment for each brand. There were also key human scenarios – such as unmasking a spy from another soft drinks company famous for a fluted bottle and a red can...

Part of the live theater: a spy from a rival company is unmasked

'Operation Breakthrough' had been immensely successful in unveiling Britvic Soft Drinks Ltd.'s new strategy. The next stage was to take this concept directly to the buyers.

149

client: **Britvic Soft Drinks Ltd.**
product: **Tango soft drinks**
fair: **Tango Caravan touring stores and supermarkets in UK**
duration: **3 months (April, May, June 1996)**
materials: **Standard touring caravan, video screens, interior furnishings**
total production time: **4 weeks**

Tango Caravan

The caravan's dark exterior hides the visual surprises within

In creating what was to be literally a vehicle for the new four-flavor strategy, there was an immediate time problem. The 're-engineering' of Tango had to be built on very rapidly. The support operation – aimed at buyers and managers in stores and supermarkets – was given a target of only six weeks in which to get underway.

In Real Life came up with the idea of a vehicle to travel round the UK making presentations to small groups. A caravan seemed particularly appropriate to the brand, however, building a vehicle from chassis up would have been too time-consuming. Instead, the designers bought a standard touring caravan, painted it black (the base color of the new packaging for Tango) and fitted it out with two large video screens and sofas for the presentations. The exterior was black with the Tango name only in white to preserve the shock and surprise of the interior. The decor inside is best described as camp from cyberspace, with fluorescent green and yellow round cushions, fur fabric seats and metalized walls.

client: **Britvic Soft Drinks Ltd.**

product: **Tango soft drinks**

The marketing argument was that the other three Tango flavors could be grown to the same heights as Orange Tango with evident benefits to retailers – the presentations in the caravan delivered this argument with wit and humor. The result was that sales proportions and orders jumped by over 50%.

Inside the caravan a screaming kitsch interior (top) sets the pace for presentations delivered in person and onscreen

client: **Britvic Soft Drinks Ltd.**
product: **Tango soft drinks**

fair: **Tango Tongue, outdoor touring of UK (beaches, parks)**
duration: **4 months**
materials: **Inflatable plastic**
total production time: **Approximately 13 weeks**

Tango Tongue

To complete the circle, *In Real Life* were asked to design a public event, which, like the caravan, could travel. It was planned specifically to promote the taste sensation of Apple Tango, and also to reinforce the overall brand message. Their solution was the Tango Tongue, a quivering inflated structure, something between a fairground fantasy and a human mouth, within which visitors would be invited to enjoy the drink – and the concept of **'seduction'** – for themselves. As with the caravan, the Tongue had no exterior branding. It would simply appear – on a holiday beach, or in a festival park – and invite the curious to explore. Once inside a whole series of objects, displays and interactive events would create a world of sensation – physical, tactile and auditory – reinforcing the concept that Apple Tango was sensuous and seductive.

Entrance to the Tango Tongue

'Introduce half a million people to the taste of Apple Tango by the end of the summer': that was the brief.

Final assembly drawing of the Tango Tongue

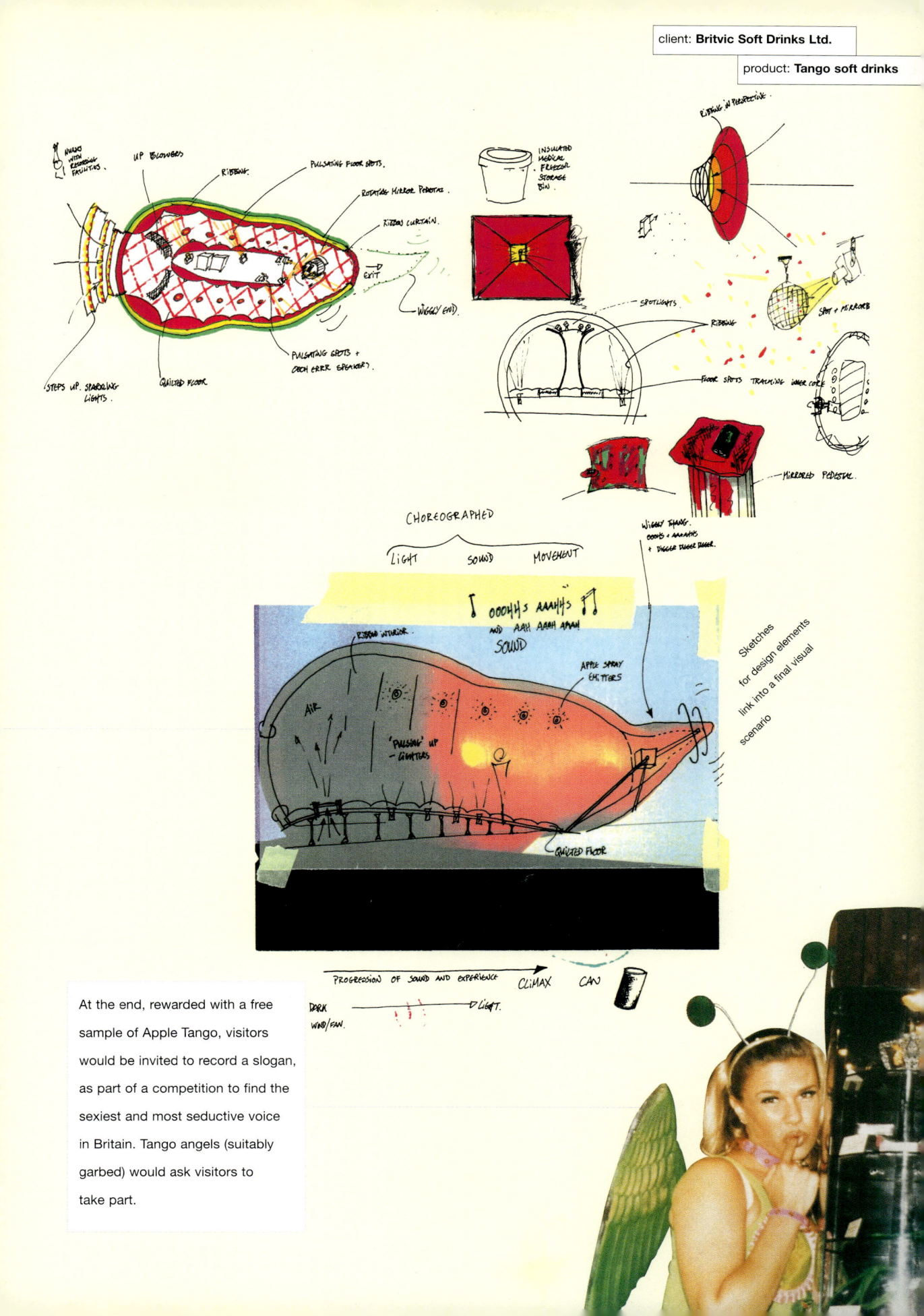

client: **Britvic Soft Drinks Ltd.**

product: **Tango soft drinks**

Sketches for design elements link into a final visual scenario

At the end, rewarded with a free sample of Apple Tango, visitors would be invited to record a slogan, as part of a competition to find the sexiest and most seductive voice in Britain. Tango angels (suitably garbed) would ask visitors to take part.

client: **Britvic Soft Drinks Ltd.**

product: **Tango soft drinks**

'We deliver design face to face.'

A key concept in marketing today is segmentation, which says that the old broad groupings of markets (by age, income, social class or whatever) are too wide, and that target audiences or consumers must be more narrowly defined. One new definition is **the segment of one**: the product must address the potential consumer personally, as an individual not just as a member of a group. In Real Life's approach to Britvic Soft Drinks Ltd. can be seen as an increasing definition of this concept. Firstly the sales conference, presenting a unique event to a chosen group, then the caravan offering a special event to two or three key buyers, then the individual swoop of the Tango angels on those taking part in the Tongue.

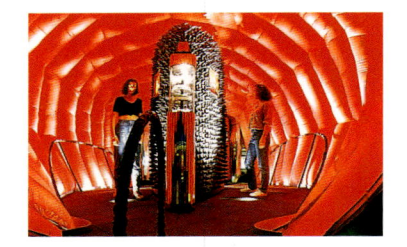

In Real Life are the ideal team to deliver such a direct message. Their creative ethos is based on delivering design human face to human face. Live media are their speciality. But their deeper understanding of their craft allows them to mold particular – not to say outrageous – solutions to a **clear vision** of the client's needs and to the brief. The Tango Tongue is an extraordinary piece of design. It is not a solution that can be applied generally, and it breaks most of the so-called rules: no exterior signage, no formal structure, no signposted marketing message. But it works because In Real Life knew how to break the rules creatively in order to meet the client's real needs.

The range of skills deployed by In Real Life are not just creative, either. The structure of the Tongue has to be safe, meeting fire and other regulations, for example; it had to be easily transported and assembled, and the accompanying team of angels and actors had to be planned and rehearsed. This demanded technical and organizational skills of a keen level, since the high public profile of the event meant that at each installation it had to be faultless. This technical expertise ran down to such mundane matters as assuring that the supply of samples would not run out, that the warm air pumped into the Tongue to add to the sensational experience would always be correctly scented, and that the tapes and documents collected each time (in themselves key marketing data) would be delivered and analyzed.

The Tango caravan was among the finalists for a Design **Effectiveness** Award in 1996, and was highly praised by the judges. This public acclaim underlines the success of In Real Life's work for their client.

ACKNOWLEDGMENTS

This book is for J., L., H. and D.

This book would not have been possible without the contribution of the designers whose work is shown here. Often very busy people, they took time to discuss not only their own projects, but also their ideas about how expo stand design should be achieved. This process for me of looking and learning was very enjoyable, and I am extremely grateful to them all.

Many thanks therefore to Geoff Aldridge, Clive Andrews, Jennifer Atkins, Paige Dunsmore, Adrian Caddy, Rachel Clare, Jo Cupper, Dejan Cehulic, Russ Fowler, Roger Frampton, Karen George, William Kauffmann, Jenny King, Liz Morgan, Wayne Newall, Kunio Ogawa, Kousaka Toshiyuki, Todd Parnell, Michael V. Parrott, Betty Pippert, Rob Quisenberry, Martin Root, Keiji Shigi, Reiko Takemura, Kevin Stokes, Maggie Templeman, Geoff Thatcher, Susan Riese, Dan Vander Sanden and Vero & Didou.

Special thanks also to Angie Patchell, to the team at The Design Revolution, and in particular to Natalia Price-Cabrera, for all their help.

Conway Lloyd Morgan, London, 1997

List of Designers

Can-Can Presentations, 47 Darwin Court, Gloucester Avenue, Regent's Park, London NW1 7BQ, UK

Communication by Design, 6 The Courthouse, 38 Kingsland Road, London E2 8DD, UK

Denby Associates, Princeton, New Jersey, USA

Derse Exhibits, 1234 North 62nd Street, Milwaukee, WI 53213-2996, USA

Architetto Pietro-Ferruccio Laviani, via Solferino 11, 20121 Milan, Italy

Fujiya Co. Ltd., Tokyo, Japan

ICON Incorporated, 8333 Clinton Park Drive, P. O. Box 10240, Fort Wayne, IN 46851-0240, USA

Imagination, South Crescent, Store Street, London WC1E 7BL, UK

Innervisions Interiors and Exhibitions Ltd., No.1, Primrose Mews, 1A Sharpleshall Street, London NW1 8YW, UK

In Real Life, 1–5 Poland Street, London W1V 4QE, UK

Kauffmann Theilig & Partner, Freie Architekten BDA, Zeppelin Strasse 10, 73760 Ostfildern-Kemnat, Germany

Marketplace Design Partnership Ltd., Pulpit House, One the Square, Abingdon, Oxfordshire OX14 5SZ, UK

MIK Planning Inc., Kioicho TBR 4F, 5–7 Kojimachi, Chiyoda-Ku, Tokyo 102, Japan

Perfectum Expo Team, Hrelic 39, 1000 Zagreb, Croatia

Phoenix Presentations, 9345 Princeton-Glendale Road, Hamilton, Ohio 45011-9707, USA

Powerhouse Exhibits & Technical Models, 9455 Waples Street, Suite 100, San Diego, CA 92121, USA

RedFish Communications Ltd., 1st Floor, 46 Old Compton Street, London W1V 5PB, UK

Root Associates, 17 Blossom Street, London E1 6PL, UK

Rouse-Wyatt Associates, 10/14 Vine Street, Cincinnati, Ohio, USA

Vero & Didou, 3 rue de la Cavée, 92140 Clamart, France

Toni Zuccheri, Via A Moro 4, 33077 Sanvito Al Tagllamento, Italy

GENERAL INDEX

Bricker, Mike **60**

Cavanagh, Lyle **48**

Client activity

communications **63–66, 107–114**

computer software and hardware **43–46, 87–92, 99–106**

consumer electronics **47–54**

drinks, food and catering **137–142, 145–154**

environmental products **27–30**

furniture, floor and wall coverings **35–41, 81–86**

glass manufacturing **125–130**

industrial equipment **59–62**

leisure, books and computer games **71–74, 75–79, 115–123, 131–136**

lighting **23–26, 67–70**

motor vehicles **12–21, 93–98**

sports goods **31–34, 55–58**

Design Awards **59–62, 63–66, 71–74, 145–154**

Ekki **35–40**

England, Carl **64**

HHCL & Partners **146**

King, Jenny **45–46**

Live participants **12–21, 87–92, 107–114, 115–123, 131–136, 145–154**

Martin, Jim **60, 62**

Meroform construction system **34**

Moss Engineering **65**

Outreach activities **93–98, 99–106, 107–114**

Pico Ltd. **118, 123**

Quisenberry, Rob **27, 29**

Reebok **31–34**

Root, Martin **123**

Smithsonian Institution **99–106**

Stand types

aisle **23–26, 67–70**

combination stand/aisle **27–30, 31–34**

enclosed **67–70, 71–74, 75–79, 99–106, 115–123**

island **12–21, 35–41, 43–46, 47–54, 55–58, 59–62, 63–66, 81–86, 87–92, 93–98, 107–114**

mobile **131–136, 145–154**

multiple application **12–21, 47–54, 87–92**

permanent **125–130, 137–142**

Szubiak, Jan **51**

Tango **145–154**

Teadt, Michael **61**

Umbro **31–34**

Video and multimedia support **12–21, 43–46, 71–74, 93–98, 99–106, 115–123, 125–130, 131–136, 137–142, 145–154**

INDEX OF DESIGNERS AND CLIENTS

America OnLine **63–66**

Azur Environmental **27–30**

Britvic Soft Drinks Ltd. **145–154**

Can-Can Presentations **43–46**

Communication by Design **125–130**

Denby Associates **99–106**

Derse Exhibits **71–74**

Emašport **31–34**

Ericsson Mobile Communications **107–114**

Ford of Europe **12–21**

Fox Video **131–136**

Fujiya Co. Ltd. **55–58**

Gardner Merchant plc **137–142**

Golden Books Family Entertainment **71–74**

GT Interactive **75–79**

Hoxan Co. **35–41**

ICON Incorporated **47–54, 59–62**

Imagination **12–21, 107–114**

In Real Life **145–154**

Innervisions Interiors and Exhibitions Ltd. **87–92**

Intel **99–106**

Kartell S.p.A. **81–86**

Kauffmann Theilig & Partner **93–98**

Laviani, Pietro-Ferruccio **81–86**

Marketplace Design **137–142**

Mercedes-Benz **93–98**

Microsoft Ltd. **87–92**

MIK Planning Inc. **35–41**

Mizuno Corporation **55–58**

Olivetti Personal Computers **43–46**

Perfectum Expo Team **31–34**

Philips Consumer Electronics **47–54**

Phoenix Presentations **63–66**

Pilkington plc **125–130**

Powerhouse Exhibits **27–30**

RedFish Communications Ltd. **131–136**

Reggiani Spa Illuminazione **67–70**

Root Associates **75–79, 115–123**

Rouse-Wyatt Associates **99–106**

Trinova Corporation **59–62**

Vero & Didou **23–26**

Vickers Division, Trinova Corporation (*see Trinova*)

Virgin Interactive Entertainment **115–123**

Zuccheri, Toni **67–70**